Tanya —
Best wishes!

signature

SERVICE INNOVATION

SERVICE INNOVATION

HOW TO GO FROM CUSTOMER NEEDS TO BREAKTHROUGH SERVICES

LANCE A. BETTENCOURT

New York   Chicago   San Francisco   Lisbon   London   Madrid   Mexico City
Milan   New Delhi   San Juan   Seoul   Singapore   Sydney   Toronto

Copyright © 2010 by The McGraw-Hill Companies, Inc. All rights reserved. Printed in the United States of America. Except as permitted under the United States Copyright Act of 1976, no part of this publication may be reproduced or distributed in any form or by any means, or stored in a database or retrieval system, without the prior written permission of the publisher.

1 2 3 4 5 6 7 8 9 0   WFR/WFR 1 5 4 3 2 1 0

ISBN 978-0-07-171300-9
MHID 0-07-171300-X

McGraw-Hill books are available at special quantity discounts to use as premiums and sales promotions or for use in corporate training programs. To contact a representative, please e-mail us at bulksales@mcgraw-hill.com.

This book is printed on acid-free paper.

Library of Congress Cataloging-in-Publication Data

Bettencourt, Lance.
    Service innovation: how to go from customer needs to breakthrough services /
By Lance Bettencourt—1st ed.
        p.   cm.
    Includes bibliographical references and index.
    ISBN-13: 978-0-07-171000-9 (alk. paper)
    1. Customer services.   2. Customer services—Technological innovations.   I. Title.

HF5415.5.B4848   2010
658.8912—dc22   2010001200

To my loving wife, Jolene,
and my four wonderful children,
Megan, Jake, Kate, and Julia.

CONTENTS

FOREWORD

Anthony W. Ulwick
Founder and CEO, Strategyn, Inc.

I have been studying and advancing the innovation process for over 20 years. If there is one thing I have learned, it is that success and efficiency at innovation are dependent on a company's ability to understand all the needs of customers in carefully chosen markets *before* attempting to generate ideas that address those needs. And yet, even today, in most companies, managers allow the organization to take an ideas-first approach—which means they are going about innovation backward. This approach is nothing more than guesswork and will never lead to an efficient innovation process.

Over the years I have also observed that although innovation in the product realm and innovation in the service realm are fundamentally the same process, there are special features of each that, if understood, can make the process more fruitful.

Lance Bettencourt understands both the necessity of a needs-first approach to innovation and how the special factors at play in services affect the pursuit of innovation in that area. *Service Innovation* offers readers far-reaching insight into both. Few people can match Lance's hands-on practitioner experience. In the seven years he has worked with me at Strategyn, he has helped our innovation theory evolve, and he understands how to put that theory into practice in any service organization.

Service Innovation describes an effective and world-class end-to-end service innovation process. The question is—is your company ready for it? Many companies still live in the world of innovation denial. They deny the fact that they face an innovation problem. They deny that the current approach to service innovation could ever be improved in a dramatic way. The companies that will benefit most from this book are the ones that have moved beyond denial and are searching for an effective service innovation process to adopt.

Exactly what does adoption mean? Companies often fear that adopting new processes means embracing broad cultural changes, which can be both time consuming and expensive. But adoption of an effective innovation process does not require broad cultural change. It merely requires management to think differently about innovation and to support an effective approach to it. Service innovation is—or should be—the responsibility of the market and service planners and strategists. They are the people who decide what offerings to create and deliver. If senior management entrusts and empowers those individuals and supplies them with the needed tools and training, the innovation process can be effectively managed and controlled by just a dozen or so people in smaller Fortune 1000 firms and by the same number in divisions of larger companies.

Companies that adopt the thinking laid out in this book will succeed at innovation. Why am I so confident? Unlike many business books, this book is not based on a theory that worked once or twice and is untested elsewhere. The concepts Lance explains in this book have been tested and refined through application in hundreds of companies over many years. They work—not just in one company or one industry, but anywhere and everywhere.

Innovation is the key to success and growth in an organization; it needs and deserves to be treated like the business process it is. This book is a giant step forward in the service arena. Once your company adopts this thinking, it will be in a great position to fine-tune its existing service offerings and secure, grow, and sustain its core businesses. It will also be able to devise new service offerings in new and emerging markets.

One thing I have truly enjoyed over the years is watching like-minded innovators such as Lance build, test, and refine the theories that have transformed innovation into a science. I encourage others to help us continue to transform the jobs-to-be-done innovation theory into practice.

ACKNOWLEDGMENTS

My passion for services marketing and management began 20 years ago when I was a student at California State University, Bakersfield. At CSUB, I was fortunate enough to take a class in services marketing taught by Dennis Guseman, now dean at California State University, San Marcos. That class was ahead of its time, and it got me interested not only in services as a work domain but also as a business area in which I could contribute my thinking.

My enthusiasm for services continued in the Ph.D. program at Arizona State University. There I had the good fortune to work with true leaders in the field of services marketing and management, including Steve Brown and Mary Jo Bitner. The Center for Services Leadership at ASU is still the leading voice for advancing services research and education. The center and the marketing department at ASU afforded me many opportunities to develop knowledge and skills that have benefited me throughout my career, for which I am very grateful.

My thinking has been shaped as profoundly by my work with Strategyn. In 2003, while I was teaching at Indiana University, Strategyn's CEO, Tony Ulwick, decided to give an academic a try. I am forever grateful for his decision. Tony laid the foundation for the approach to service innovation that I describe in this book, and he and I have continued to advance this thinking together.

Within Strategyn, I also deeply appreciate my wonderful consulting colleagues, including Sandy Bates, Jeff Baker, Eric Eskey, Mark Jaster, Michael Lee, Zac Lyons, Rick Norman, Bob Pennisi, Rob Schade, Urko Wood, and the international Strategyn consulting team. They have contributed in many ways to the thinking shared in this book. I also owe special thanks to Francesca Forrest for her exceptional freelance editing of the book.

Although I have worked with many incredible clients, I would like to thank specifically several who have contributed directly to the thinking and content of this book, including Angelo Rago of Abbott Medical Optics; Dave Wascha of Microsoft; Andrea Johnson and Ben Allen of Kroll; Julie Lutz, Jay Johnson, and Jeff Hynds of Ingersoll-Rand; Lance Reschke of Ceridian; Philicia Belzycki Cohen of TD Bank; Wade Powell of Lexmark; Eric Whipkey of the Society for Human Resource Management; Craig Libby, formerly of Wachovia; Liz Alchimio of State Farm; and Michael Reynolds of Wellpoint.

Finally, I offer my thanks to my amazing wife and children to whom this book is dedicated. They are the loves of my life. To my parents, my brother and sister and their families, and my friends, you mean so much to me. And last in the list but first in importance, I am grateful to God for every opportunity I have, every skill I have been given, and every day that I live.

INTRODUCTION
SERVICE INNOVATION: FROM CONFUSION TO CLARITY

Services dominate our economy and everyday life.[1] Though I have been studying services for two decades now, I am still a bit amazed when I look through a list of business sectors and see just how many are services and how important these industries are to the overall U.S. and global economy. According to economic census figures from 2007, more than 80 percent of the U.S. gross domestic product derives from service industries.[2] Well over 80 percent of employees in the United States work in service industries. And similar statistics can be found in other developed countries as well.

These service industries include education, construction, health care, utilities, retail and wholesale trade, finance and insurance, real estate, hospitality, transportation, entertainment, and a whole host of other personal and professional services. In addition, most companies that offer products for sale also offer services. IBM, for example, offers consulting services, and Hewlett-Packard offers financial services.

Given the dominance of service industries in the economy, it makes sense that people are interested in how to manage them properly. Over the past three decades, many excellent books have been written about services strategy, management, marketing, and operations. Several universities have developed curricula devoted to services. And research centers such as the Center for Services Leadership at Arizona State University and professional associations such as the Information Technology Services Marketing Association have grown in significance.

Yet, there is still one nagging area of confusion that demands attention—service innovation. Innovation is a top priority for service executives, but they lack the guidance required to innovate in a meaningful way. As noted innovation expert Henry Chesbrough lamented just a few years ago, there is a "problem of innovation in services." Chesbrough pondered, "Without tangible products to prototype and focus on, how can we determine whether we're designing what customers want?"[3]

Most service executives ask themselves the same question. In 2007, IBM and Oracle formed a nonprofit consortium focused on service research and innovation—the Service Research & Innovation Institute. One of its key objectives is to bring together industry, academic, and government partners to advance understanding of the innovation of services. Describing the impetus for founding the nonprofit consortium, Jim Spohrer, a director of service research at IBM, noted, "People have a good idea of what technological innovation is. But service innovation is more hidden."[4] The absence of guidance on service innovation means that for more than 80 percent of U.S. companies, there is a hole in management understanding of one of the most critical functions of a business.

The dearth of insight into meaningful service innovation is remarkable when one considers the potential of service innovation to drive revenues and shape entire industries. Consider the success of MinuteClinic, a minimal-wait, walk-in health clinic service. Founded in 2000, MinuteClinic now has more than 500 locations in 25 states. What accounts for its success?

MinuteClinics treat a limited number of common ailments, are conveniently located near where their customers live, are open seven days a week, and never require an appointment. This makes them ideal for anyone seeking fast and affordable access to medical diagnoses and care for everyday ailments that might otherwise go untreated due to lack of insurance, high costs, need for an appointment, and other related concerns. In other words, MinuteClinic offers a highly differentiated service that satisfies some very distinct unmet customer needs.

The absence of a clear model to guide service innovation success can also be quite costly. More than 4 out of 10 new services fail, and this statistic must be interpreted in light of the fact that the development of truly new services is rare.[5] Among the many negatives of new service failures are lost investments, lost customer goodwill, and potential damage to the corporate brand image. Without exception, studies of new service success versus failure point to the vital importance of having a well-differentiated service concept built on a solid understanding of customer needs. And there's the rub: how can you gain that understanding and craft a well-differentiated concept?

Confusion Reigns

Unfortunately, most attempts to offer guidance only add to the confusion. For one thing, most management teams fail to distinguish between service innovation and service development.[6] *Service innovation* is the process of devising a new or improved service concept that satisfies the customer's unmet needs. Service development, in contrast, occurs once a service concept has been devised. *Service development* refers to all the activities involved in bringing that concept to market.[7] Innovation experts may disagree on where innovation—creation of a new concept—ends and development begins, but they agree that innovation entails the generation and detailed description of valuable concepts based on an understanding of customer needs. They also agree that companies often lack processes for these critical front-end activities, and this leads to the high failure rate for new services.

Because people confuse service innovation with service development, guidance is offered that fails to provide insight into the fundamentals of service innovation: uncovering customer needs and devising innovative service concepts. It's only by knowing what customers need that companies can engage in meaningful new service creation, but this is where so many companies falter.

For example, in an article entitled "R&D Comes to Services," Stefan Thomke offers some valuable advice pertaining to service development and testing.[8] However, he also offers a five-step model for service innovation that raises more questions than it answers. The first step calls for the "evaluation of ideas." But where did these ideas come from? How were the customer needs that presumably led to the development of these ideas captured? More generally, executives are left wondering: How could customer needs have been captured that could have led to service innovations such as MinuteClinic, PayPal, and Facebook? What types of customer needs should a company capture to guide the development of next-generation health care services, consulting services, and financial services? Once customer needs are known, how can innovative service concepts be formulated?

A second problem with much of the advice available on service innovation is its undue focus on the service itself and the unique characteristics of services. This may seem like an odd statement in a book about service innovation, but it is true nonetheless. Let me explain.

Service innovation must begin with the recognition that services are solutions to customer needs. They are a means to an end, not an end in themselves. I don't need a doctor, a physical exam, or a prescription. What I need is diagnosis and treatment for an illness. The emergence of WebMD and self-diagnostics such as home pregnancy tests is witness to this fact. And here is a key truth: as long as service innovation remains fixated on particular services, innovation will be constrained because the focus will be on the means instead of the end. What is the point of improving a current service when you are still not sure what customers are trying to achieve? How likely are you to come up with entirely new service offerings when the anchor point is a current service?

A focus on the service itself has led to considerable emphasis on developing tools such as service experience design—as if these tools were synonymous with service innovation. These tools are designed to improve customers' experiences with a company's existing services. I cannot deny the importance of good service experiences. Personally, I love them. But the focus is all wrong if one is seeking to create new services. Let's be perfectly clear: nobody goes to a bank in order to have a good experience with the bank. They may select Bank A over Bank B because Bank A delivers a better experience, but let's not confuse that with why a person uses a bank in the first place. What someone seeking service innovation in the banking sector should be asking is, why does anyone use the services of a bank or financial service provider? Why might they? What are the challenges and struggles that customers encounter while trying to accomplish these goals?

Ironically, an overemphasis on the unique characteristics of services has caused service innovation to fall into the trap that has plagued product innovation for decades: capturing requirements on the solution rather than customer needs. Mystery shoppers, transaction satisfaction surveys, and annual quality surveys are all means of uncovering customers' perceptions of service quality, which, once obtained, are then used as a key input into service innovation initiatives. But these tools are focused on current services, not on customers' underlying needs. Thus, they offer limited insight for the innovation of new services.

It is true that there are important differences between goods and services: services are more intangible than goods; services are often produced and consumed at the same time; quality control is more difficult because many services involve employees and customers as part of the product; services cannot be inventoried. But these differences are more relevant when it comes to the management of services than to the innovation of services, though they do play an important role in service concept design that will be described in this book. Unfortunately, undue attention to the unique nature of services has actually constrained past thinking about how to approach service innovation. With the substantial role that services play in our economy, it is time to take service innovation to a new level.

From Confusion to Clarity

Services that provide distinctive value to customers have more than three times the success rate of me-too services. And services that clearly align with customer needs achieve more than five times the success rate of services that have a poor fit with customer needs.[9] In other words, successful service innovation begins with a proper understanding of customer needs.

Most companies, unfortunately, do not understand what customer needs they should capture to guide service innovation or how to uncover them. Without proper customer inputs, companies are likely to end up with incremental me-too service improvements, high service failure rates, general confusion about what new services to offer, and poor execution due to cross-functional misalignment. But it doesn't have to be this way.

For the past seven years, I have helped clients in a variety of industries to apply an approach to innovation that is as relevant to service innovation as it is to the innovation of tangible goods. This approach is *outcome-driven innovation*, an innovation philosophy and process built around the understanding that people "hire" goods and services to get jobs done.[10] We hire a nutrition plan to prepare healthy meals. We hire a search engine to locate information. We hire a real estate agent to buy or sell a home. We hire a storage facility to store goods. We hire a financial planner to develop a financial plan. And I could give many more examples.

A focus on the customer job offers several benefits to service innovation. First, and most important, when you focus on the customer job, your understanding of customer value is no longer limited by preconceived notions about a solution because your focus is no longer on the solution. It takes the focus off the service, and places it squarely on what the customer is trying to accomplish. This means that value can be defined from a customer perspective in a manner that can guide not only improvements to current services but also the creation of entirely new services (what some refer to as *radical service innovation*).

Second, when the focus is on the customer job, you can rely on customers to inform you of their needs for service innovation. This flies in the face of what you may hear from many so-called experts, who say that customers do not know what they need and cannot articulate their needs even if they can identify them. This is simply not true once the focus is placed on the customer job rather than on service requirements: customers know very well what they are trying to get done and can explain quite clearly how they measure success in accomplishing a job.[11]

Third, a focus on the customer job provides a broader and deeper understanding of customer needs to guide service innovation. In addition to discovering other jobs that the customer is trying to get done, a company can deconstruct a specific customer job and search for opportunities at each step. This process may reveal particular steps that have been previously overlooked. It is also sure to uncover difficulties that customers have with particular steps. Those difficulties—those places where the outcomes customers use to measure success are poorly satisfied—may present service innovation opportunities that the company would otherwise overlook.

Fourth, by focusing on the customer job, companies gain a better understanding of substitutes and competitive threats, and how to innovate against them. Services don't just compete with other services; they compete with anything the customer might use or do to get the job done better. Forewarned is forearmed: with a job focus, a company can determine how to compete with both its close (other services) and far (substitutes) competitors because the customer job transcends solutions. For example, using a single set of customer outcomes (customers' metrics of success in getting a job done), a tax prep service could identify its strengths and weaknesses in comparison with those of other retail services, a certified public accountant, tax prep software, or the combination of paper, pencil, and calculator.

Finally, a focus on the customer job enables a company to discover innovation opportunities that appeal to a broader set of potential customers. A customer job not only transcends competitive offerings; it also transcends users and nonusers of market solutions. Currently, we are speaking with a financial services client about how to discover opportunities to innovate in a way that appeals to both banking and nonbanking customers who are trying to save money. Both banking and nonbanking customers are trying to get the job of saving money done, and the outcomes they use to measure success are useful for innovation regardless of how customers currently get the job done.

Once a company understands the type of information it needs from customers in order to innovate and how to capture that information, it is in a much better position to create services that customers really value. It will finally be able to identify opportunities for meaningful service innovation in a systematic and repeatable manner. Ultimately, it will be positioned for market leadership.

Take the case of Kroll Ontrack, a technology services division of the risk consultancy firm Kroll. In the late 1990s, it had started a small business focused on electronic document discovery for the legal industry. However, it lacked a strategy for growth built on what its clients wanted to achieve. By focusing on lawyers' jobs of managing information throughout the litigation process (including steps such as initial disclosure, discovery, trial, and post-trial activities) and discovering electronic documents related to a case (including steps such as capturing information, searching information, and modifying the information), Kroll Ontrack gained the insight it required. Lawyers were asked to prioritize the outcomes associated with each step for these jobs: that is, they were asked how important each outcome was and how satisfied they were with their ability to achieve each outcome. Using that information, Kroll Ontrack developed a product strategy road map that has guided the innovation of specific services, such as consulting guidance, and enabling technologies, such as clever search algorithms.

Kroll Ontrack's strategy and approach to innovation has certainly paid off. It has grown from $11 million in electronic discovery revenues in 2001 to over $200 million in 2008, and the company is the industry leader in both market share and revenues. In contrast, a myopic definition of the market ultimately cost the leading competitors their discovery business. As Ben

Allen, CEO of Kroll and former Kroll Ontrack president, explains, "If these big, well-established companies had understood the outcomes that customers really valued, they could have dominated this business. I think they saw themselves as paper document processing companies, not discovery solutions providers. The leaders today—none of them were players in the old paper discovery business."[12]

Where Do We Go from Here?

With the customer job as its starting point, this book offers a detailed consideration of the types of customer needs that can guide service innovation, how to uncover them, and how to create innovative service concepts that provide distinctive value to customers. At every point, this book offers practical guidance for the so-called fuzzy front end of service innovation.

The book starts with discovering service innovation opportunities, and then it moves through designing unique and valuable concepts. In the first part of the book, we consider specific frameworks for discovering service innovation opportunities, based on a detailed understanding of customer needs. The first five chapters of the book explain how to discover opportunities for new service innovation (helping customers get more jobs done); core service innovation (helping customers get a core job done better); service delivery innovation (helping customers to have a better experience obtaining service benefits); and supplementary service innovation (helping customers to get the most value out of owning and using a product). The remaining chapters explain how to design breakthrough service concepts to satisfy customer needs.

Chapter 1, "Customer Needs That Drive Service Innovation," discusses several fundamental truths about customer needs.

These truths lay the foundation for uncovering different types of service innovation opportunities. Specifically, we focus on the two types of customer needs that guide service innovation: the need to get a job done and the need to obtain a satisfactory outcome for each step in the execution of the job. Finally, a framework is presented to help companies go from a desire to innovate to unique and valuable service concepts.

Chapter 2, "Discover Opportunities for New Service Innovation," explains how a company can uncover more jobs that might be satisfied by its services. This chapter offers a powerful perspective on uncovering new service opportunities, a key area of struggle for so many companies. Distinct types of jobs that may provide the foundation for new service innovation are introduced, along with guidance on how to uncover these jobs.

Chapter 3, "Discover Opportunities for Core Service Innovation," introduces a universal job map for uncovering opportunities to help customers get a specific core job done better—often the primary reason for which current services are hired. This framework helps companies both to understand the outcomes that customers use to evaluate current services and to identify innovation opportunities related to those outcomes. The opportunities may lead to improvements in a current service, but they are not limited to this. The job map also reveals natural adjacencies for new products and services to complement current services.

Chapter 4, "Discover Opportunities for Service Delivery Innovation," introduces a universal job map of the steps that a customer goes through when obtaining service from a company. Unlike the job map presented in Chapter 3, the job map presented here explicitly acknowledges that the solution the customer is using is a service. The job map for obtaining service provides clear guidance that a company can act on to improve the design of a current service. Even in this chapter, however, a specific form of service is not assumed (for example, Internet, in person); a company can still gain rich insight into opportunities to create value through innovative new ways to deliver a given service.

Chapter 5, "Discover Opportunities for Supplementary Service Innovation," shows companies how to discover opportunities for new and improved services that support core product offerings. The insights of this chapter are essential not only for companies wanting to understand the design opportunities associated with support services but also for companies wanting to develop new revenue-generating services to support current product offerings.

Chapter 6, "Discover Opportunities for Service Delivery Innovation: The Provider Perspective," complements the perspective offered in Chapter 4 by introducing a universal job map for providing service. The universal job map introduced in this chapter charts each of the steps a company must take for any service to be successful. It can help a company design innovative services and discover opportunities from the perspective of the company's internal customers (its employees) by prompting the company to think through all of the elements necessary for providing a successful service.

Chapter 7, "Discover Ways to Differentiate Service Delivery," presents a comprehensive model of strategic design options available when designing or redesigning a service. The model introduces the key elements of differentiation in service delivery innovation, providing a framework for executives who are seeking to create truly breakthrough service concepts—those that deliver value to customers and the company. The chapter also shows how, by superimposing the model onto the job map for providing service, managers can create a detailed design for a service concept.

Chapter 8, "Define Innovative Service Concepts," describes the structure and elements a company must consider when defining a new or improved service concept. Services are different, and this is the point in the innovation process when the unique characteristics of services come front and center. Specific guidance is offered in this chapter for how to define innovative service concepts that will deliver the value customers are seeking.

In addition to the chapters focused on service innovation, I have included a brief conclusion that considers the relevance of the approach presented in this book to innovation more broadly.

Many companies operate under the unfortunate and misguided belief that innovation is inherently disorganized and cannot be structured. This misconception is especially prevalent among service company executives. After all, they reason, we are dealing with intangibles. But that's a red herring: service innovation, like product innovation, can be organized and predictable. The chapters that follow outline a systematic and repeatable approach to service innovation that I hope will dispel that misconception once and for all.

Over the past decade, my colleagues and I have helped numerous service companies apply outcome-driven innovation to their businesses. We have worked with clients across a variety of service industries, including insurance (for example, State Farm, Anthem); financial services (for example, Toronto Dominion Bank, H&R Block); information services (for example, Elsevier, Trend Micro); B2B professional services (for example, Ceridian, Cintas); and many others. In addition, we have helped clients best known for the goods they offer to identify service innovation opportunities (for example, Abbott Medical Optics, Ingersoll-Rand). The approach we have developed through those experiences is the one outlined in this book. I am confident that it can take service innovation in your business to a new level.

SERVICE INNOVATION

CHAPTER 1

CUSTOMER NEEDS THAT DRIVE SERVICE INNOVATION

The secret of true service innovation is that you must shift the focus away from the service solution and back to the customer. Rather than asking, "How are we doing?" a company must ask, "How is the customer doing?" To achieve this shift in focus, companies must begin to think very differently about how customers define value based on the needs they are trying to satisfy. A proper understanding of these needs enables value to be understood in advance of any particular innovation being created. True service innovation demands that a company expand its horizon beyond existing services and service capabilities and give its attention to the jobs that customers are trying to get done and the outcomes that they use to measure success in completing those jobs.

The best guide to discovering service innovation opportunities is knowing how customers define value and the types of customer needs that can direct meaningful service innovation.[1] This chapter begins by considering four truths about how service customers define value and then presents four approaches companies can take to discover service innovation opportunities. It concludes by discussing how a company can go from a desire to innovate to a specific service strategy built around a unique and valuable service concept.

1

How Do Service Customers Define Value?

How do service customers define value? Few companies know the answer, and, lacking this knowledge, they are missing an essential ingredient to service innovation success. There are four fundamental truths related to customer needs that provide the answer to this question. These four truths provide a basis for the systematic discovery of opportunities for unique and valuable service innovations.

1. Customers Hire Products and Services to Get a Job Done

We hire a credit card to make purchases. We hire a doctor to diagnose and treat an illness. We hire education to develop career skills. We hire a home builder to build a home. We hire a trucking company to transport goods. We hire support services to troubleshoot an equipment malfunction.

When we consider services in terms of the job the customer is trying to get done rather than in terms of the service itself, then our definition of value no longer is tied to current services. The customer doesn't value any particular service solution; what the customer values is the ability to get the job done well. The customer job therefore offers a stable, long-term focal point for either the improvement of current services *or* the creation of new-to-the-world services. Ultimately, customers are loyal to the job, and they will migrate to whatever solutions help them to get the job done better.

Consider how this change in focus would affect credit card innovation. A traditional innovation focus for a credit card company would be the card itself. The company would host interviews with customers and ask what they liked and disliked about their credit card. They might even ask what improvements customers would like to see. With this approach, it's all about the card, and the insights would be about the card—for example, the company would likely discover that customers want low interest rates, don't want to have their card rejected, desire fraud protection, and so on.

In contrast, when the focus is placed upon the job for which a credit card is hired—making purchases—a whole new domain of customer needs opens up. The company can now discover that customers struggle with finding desired products to purchase, choosing among competing brands, tracking purchase spending, and a whole host of other steps required to get this job done. With the wealth of data that a credit card company already has at its disposal, it is in a perfect position to help customers overcome their difficulties in many of these other areas. For instance, a credit card company might be able to link its card into the self-serve price scanners at stores such as Target to provide customers with in-store customer ratings of different brands of a given product that they are interested in purchasing.

In addition, a focus on customer jobs would enable the company to discover related jobs that customers are trying to get done, such as keeping track of warranties, tracking spending while traveling, and even controlling impulse buying. Any one of these or other related jobs could lead to new credit card services. This is the power of making the job, rather than the service, the unit of analysis.

2. Customers Hire Solutions to Accomplish Distinct Steps in Getting an Entire Job Done

A job is a process, and any step in that process presents opportunities for innovation, but many services offer value to customers for only certain steps. For example, most credit card companies focus all their attention on the paying step. They neglect the various other steps along the way in the job of making purchases—steps such as choosing from among competing brands (which comes before paying) or tracking purchase spending (which comes after paying). The result is that many companies leave value opportunities on the table, opportunities that are adjacent to what they currently offer. When a company looks at the complete job the customer is trying to get done by hiring its service, it is in a much better position to optimize its core service offering or to create entirely new services in what might be considered adjacent markets.

It also helps to realize that customers must accomplish a universal set of steps to be successful in getting a job done. We'll go over these steps in more detail in Chapter 3, but they include defining goals and resource needs for the job, locating required inputs, making the preparations or the evaluation required to get the job done, verifying readiness or choices, carrying out the core job, assessing job execution, making required adjustments, and concluding the job. For a financial investment service, a customer must define financial goals, locate investment options, evaluate investments, choose specific investments, invest finances, assess investment performance, adjust investment allocations, and store and retrieve investment information. Looked at from this perspective, there are many opportunities for service innovation.

3. Customers Use Outcomes to Evaluate Success in Getting a Job Done

Outcomes are customers' measures of how well they are able to get the job—or a step in the job—done. When customers hire products and services to get a job done, they choose from among competing solutions based on how well the various solutions satisfy the outcomes they are looking to achieve. Suppose, for example, I am trying to do the job of making a purchase. When I choose from among the options available to me for making a purchase, I will choose the option that best satisfies my high-priority outcomes, such as wanting to accomplish one or more of the following:

- Minimize the time it takes to complete the transaction
- Minimize the likelihood of buying more than needed
- Minimize the total amount paid for the purchase

As mentioned above, to get any job done, customers must go through a universal set of steps, and for each step, customers may have 5 to 10 or more outcomes that they consider important. These outcomes provide rich insight into what customers are trying to achieve, regardless of the solution hired. So, for example, in the job of preparing income taxes, customers must complete the step of determining deductions, and there are perhaps a dozen outcomes that customers use to judge how successfully they have completed that step. Customers may measure their success in determining deductions by how well they are able to accomplish the following:

- Minimize the time it takes to determine if a specific expense is deductible
- Minimize the likelihood that a legitimate deduction is overlooked
- Minimize the likelihood that a claimed deduction triggers an IRS audit

Even when there are no product or service solutions available for customers to hire, they still have outcomes against which they measure how successfully they are getting the step in the job or the overall job done. This means that the metrics that customers will use to evaluate a new service can be known in advance of the service itself being launched. So, for example, even before MinuteClinic was founded, one outcome I desired from medical care—and I'm sure most people feel similarly—was reducing the time it takes to be seen by a medical provider when I am sick. MinuteClinic just happens to address that outcome with its service. Current services are merely point-in-time solutions that enable customers to achieve the stable outcomes they use to evaluate how successfully a job is completed. This is why jobs and outcomes provide the optimal road map for service innovation.

4. Customers Have Distinct Needs That Arise Related to the "Consumption" of a Solution

On the one hand, customers have needs related to getting a job done—they are the reasons people hire a product or service. These needs include both the jobs that customers are trying to get done by hiring a service—both functional and emotional jobs—and the outcomes that customers use to evaluate success in getting a job done. Knowing these needs, a company can create entirely new service concepts and can improve current services. On the other hand, once a customer decides to hire a particular service to get a job done, there are tasks that customers must accomplish as part of "consuming" that service—things like making contact with the service, communicating service needs, and paying for the service. That is, the customer must go through a series of steps to obtain the service and receive its intended benefits. This is true whether we are talking about having a meal at a restaurant, getting a haircut, or obtaining a mortgage. Suppose I decide to hire a mortgage to buy a home. Having made this decision, I now have distinct needs related to obtaining the mortgage itself. These needs are vital considerations in how a service is designed and delivered, but unlike needs related to getting the primary job done, these needs presume a service solution.

So there is a distinction between needs that guide service concept creation and needs that guide service concept design—but that doesn't mean that one category of needs is more important than the other. A company must ultimately satisfy both types of customer needs if it is to have commercial success. For example, if customers received excellent medical treatment from MinuteClinic, but they had horrible experiences trying to pay for the service, MinuteClinic might not last long. By the same token, the best payment service is not going to save a medical provider if the medical care is inferior.

A similar distinction can be made between why products are hired and the needs that customers have once they own and are using a specific product. I hire a motorcycle for the transportation it provides. However, once I own a motorcycle, I also have needs related to learning to ride it, maintaining it, storing it, and, ultimately, selling or disposing of it.

How Can Services Create Value?

A company can choose to pursue any of four basic types of service innovation opportunity, each of which involves a slightly different approach (see Figure 1-1). The four approaches represent a comprehensive set of options for discovering service innovation opportunities by focusing both on what customers are trying to get done *and* what customers must do to "consume" a particular solution.

The four approaches to service innovation are these:

- *New service innovation.* Innovation comes from the discovery of new or related jobs that a current or new service can help the customer get done.
- *Core service innovation.* Innovation comes from helping the customer get a core job done better by improving a current service or introducing new services.

Figure 1-1   Approaches to Discovering Service Innovation Opportunities

---

NEW SERVICE INNOVATION

Objective: Discover new or related jobs that a current or new service can help the customer get done.

Focus: New or related customer jobs

CORE SERVICE INNOVATION

Objective: Discover ways to help the customer get a core job done better with new or improved services.

Focus: Outcomes on a core job for which service is hired

SERVICE DELIVERY INNOVATION

Objective: Discover ways to improve how the benefits of a service are obtained by the customer.

Focus: Outcomes on obtaining service

SUPPLEMENTARY SERVICE INNOVATION

Objective: Discover ways to help the customer with jobs related to product ownership and/or usage.

Focus: Outcomes on a specific job related to product usage or consumption

---

- *Service delivery innovation.* Innovation comes from improving how the customer obtains the benefits of a service when getting a core job done.
- *Supplementary service innovation.* Innovation comes from helping the customer get jobs related to product usage or consumption done.

In contemplating each approach, a company is forced to think about service innovation from multiple valuable perspectives. But a company shouldn't limit itself to pursuing just one approach; there is no reason not to pursue multiple approaches, and indeed, sometimes the approaches overlap. Sometimes, for example, it is hard to separate core service innovation from service delivery innovation because the only way to get the core job done is to hire a service, such as making a travel reservation. So the point of calling attention to these four types of innovation opportunity isn't to limit companies; on the contrary, it is to show them their many options. Take the case of IBM, which used to regard services primarily as a means to support its products—that is, when it thought about service innovation, it thought only of the fourth type: supplementary service innovation. In the past two decades, however, IBM has come to see the broader possibilities that service innovation offers. It has grown services revenue from $10 billion in the early 1990s to more than $50 billion today through a combined focus on all four innovation approaches.

In the coming paragraphs, we will explore what each approach has to offer. Each of the four approaches is covered in more detail in the chapter devoted to it.

New Service Innovation

We hire services to get jobs done. What's more, we hire different services to get different jobs done—and often from the same company. For example, we might hire a professional association to keep us up-to-date on current practices (webinars), give us opportunities to network with colleagues (conferences), and enable us to maintain professional certification (classes). As such, a company that is looking for opportunities to develop new services needs to uncover more jobs that it might be able to help customers accomplish.

Let's consider the case of PetSmart, which was originally a retailer (known until 1989 as PetFood Warehouse) that helped customers do the job of buying pet food. Over the years, Pet-Smart has expanded its vision to lifetime care for pets, and in doing so, it has opened up many more possible jobs that it can help customers get done via new services. Among these are a full-service salon (which helps customers with the jobs of bathing and grooming their pets), in-store vet clinics (which help customers with the jobs of vaccinating their pets and maintaining their pets' health, more generally), pet training services (which help customers with pet training and bonding), a Pets-Hotel (which helps with the job of caring for pets while customers are working), and a Smart Nutrition Selector (which helps with the job of determining what to feed a pet). Since 2000, when PetSmart adopted the vision statement "To provide Total Lifetime Care for every pet, every parent, every time" and refocused its strategy on providing services to fulfill this vision, revenue from services has grown more than 20 percent per year on average.

New service innovation focuses on uncovering new and related jobs that the customer wants to accomplish. Because jobs are independent of today's solutions, the customer may not be using a particular solution—let alone a service solution—to get the job done. All that matters is that the customer wants to get the job done. When a company collects a detailed set of jobs that customers are trying to get done, it often discovers many for which there are currently no solutions. Therefore, a focus on new and related customer jobs truly opens up a company's service innovation possibilities.

Core Service Innovation

Although a company may help customers with multiple jobs, most individual services focus on helping the customer get a core job done. Consider the following examples of jobs and services that address them:

- Improve learning skills and understanding (personal tutor)
- Diagnose a medical condition (MRI scan)
- Find a home for sale (MLS.com, an online real estate advertising service)
- Pay for a college education (529 college savings plans)
- Stay in a location away from home (hotel)
- Transport cargo (freight service)

Given the importance of the core job, it makes sense for companies to understand the struggles that customers have when using current services to get a core job done. Core service innovation often reveals opportunities for improving or extending current services, but because the focus is on the job, it can also lead to entirely new services and service models. This is especially true if the core job is defined in a manner that encompasses complementary solutions to getting the entire job done—a topic to which we will return in Chapter 3.

Since the 1990s, for example, UPS has been expanding beyond package delivery into other specialized services related to its vision of enabling global commerce. It has done this by developing service offerings focused on specific core jobs its customers are trying to get done. UPS Supply Chain Solutions, for example, has introduced consulting services that help customers to execute the various steps involved with such core jobs as designing a supply chain network, fulfilling orders, and managing postsale returns. Hired by a distributor of periodicals who needed a more efficient delivery system, for example, UPS consultants helped the distributor to understand inefficiencies in the current system, create new work standards, plan system requirements, identify and evaluate technology vendors, develop and assess a new delivery system, and oversee the full implementation of the system.

Core service innovation reveals opportunities for new and improved services by uncovering the outcomes that customers use to judge success in getting the job done. A universal job map for getting a core job done guides the job mapping process. Once customer outcomes are captured for each step, the degree to which customers are satisfied by current services (and other solutions) can be measured. Any important areas in which they are not satisfied present opportunities for innovation. And once the company has developed a new or improved service concept, it can measure how well the concept improves customers' satisfaction with their outcomes.

Service Delivery Innovation

Many companies have successfully differentiated their services on the basis of service delivery. That's what's behind Enterprise Rent-a-Car's "We'll Pick You Up" ad campaign and the classic Burger King slogan "Have It Your Way." It's also what's behind airport check-in kiosks, online banking, LiveChat with a Web retailer, and a whole host of other service innovations. In these examples, it's all about the process of obtaining the service.

The experience of Progressive illustrates the merits of this approach to service innovation. Now the number 4 auto insurance company in the United States, over the past three years, Progressive has doubled the number of new policies it writes. It has sought to differentiate its auto insurance services on the basis of how the services are received rather than on the basis of the core benefit offered. Going back more than five decades, Progressive was the first auto insurance company to offer a drive-in claims service and the option to pay premiums in installments. In the 1990s, Progressive really made a name for itself through two key service delivery innovations. In 1994, Progressive introduced its 1-800 rate comparison service: with a single call, customers could receive a Progressive auto insurance quote and comparisons with up to three competitors. That same year, Progressive also introduced its fleet of immediate-response vehicles, which brought claims professionals to the customer—even to the scene of an accident. Recent innovations have continued the focus on service delivery. In 2003, Progressive rolled out a concierge claims service, which means that a Progressive representative oversees the entire claims and repair process on behalf of the customer. More recently, Progressive has been promoting policy customization, 24/7 live support, and the option to name your price.

Service delivery innovation focuses on improving how a service is delivered to customers by uncovering the outcomes they use to judge success when obtaining service. A universal job map for the steps involved in obtaining service guides the mapping of this consumption chain job. The steps reflect what the customer must accomplish to receive the service, starting with defining service needs and then moving to making contact with the service provider and receiving and paying for the service. Once customer outcomes are captured and prioritized, a company can begin work on service delivery innovation.

Supplementary Service Innovation

In order to get the most value out of the products they hire, customers often require supplementary help. Specifically, customers may have consumption chain jobs related to selecting, purchasing, installing, learning how to use, using, moving or storing, maintaining, upgrading, and disposing of a product. In fact, the core job of many services is to help customers to accomplish consumption chain jobs related to owning and using products. This means that product companies can benefit from studying the jobs surrounding product ownership and usage: they can discover opportunities for the creation or enhancement of supplementary services. And—it is important to note—these services are supplementary only in the sense that they support product ownership and usage. Don't make the mistake of thinking that therefore they lack importance. On the contrary: for customers, supplementary services play a critical role in the overall value equation, and they are often big revenue generators for the company.

Hewlett-Packard (HP), for example, offers supplementary services for the entire ownership life cycle of the technology products it sells. HP offers installation and deployment services for their various technology products, including servers, storage devices, networking hubs, PCs, and printers. To keep things running, HP offers hardware and software support, along with repair services for cases of actual breakdowns. To help professionals learn how to get the most from the technology they are purchasing, HP offers classroom training by accredited instructors. HP also offers services to come alongside a company in order to optimize the use of technology assets. Finally, on the front end and back end of the ownership life cycle, HP offers financing services to help with making a purchase and asset recovery services to help with disposing of unwanted equipment.

Supplementary service innovation reveals opportunities for new and improved services by understanding customers' struggles related to owning and using a product. This entails uncovering the outcomes that customers are dissatisfied with as they try to get a particular consumption chain job done or as they use a product to get a core job done. As with the other types of innovation, once a company has decided which consumption chain job it wants to focus on, it must map the steps in getting the consumption chain job done and uncover the outcomes by which customers measure success in that task. The outcomes that customers rate as most important and with which they are least satisfied then become targets for innovation.

How Is a Successful Service Strategy Developed?

How does a company go from innovation and growth objectives to unique and valuable service concepts? Figure 1-2 presents the principal steps in developing a service strategy built around unmet customer needs. These steps provide a systematic and repeatable road map to service innovation. Let's consider each step in turn.

Figure 1-2   How a Successful Service Strategy Is Developed

STEP 1. SELECT THE INNOVATION FOCUS.
- Select the discovery option to pursue.
- Decide who the customer is.
- Decide upon a job or job area to investigate.

STEP 2. UNCOVER CUSTOMER NEEDS.
- Talk to the customers.
- Ask the right questions.
- Ensure quality job and outcome statements.

STEP 3. PRIORITIZE CUSTOMER NEEDS.
- Survey customers.
- Measure importance and satisfaction.
- Calculate opportunity.

STEP 4. DEVELOP A SERVICE STRATEGY.
- Define a unique and valuable position.
- Define the service concept.

Step 1. Select the Innovation Focus

A company must make three decisions regarding innovation focus. First, it must decide which of the service innovation discovery options to pursue based on its objectives. It is important to make this decision up front since it guides the approach and the type of customer needs to uncover, as indicated in Figure 1-1.

Second, a company must decide what customer group or groups to target. The customer group or groups are those who rely on the company's services to get a job done. It is those customers who are most likely to recognize the value delivered by a service. A company may want to target more than one customer group because several customer groups may rely on the company's services to get distinct jobs done, or several customer groups may participate in the accomplishment of a given job. For example, for services related to recovering lost data on a computer, data owners are one customer group, and IT managers who manage data recovery are another.

The customer group should be defined as broadly as possible. For core and new service innovation, in particular, the customer group shouldn't be restricted to those who presently hire a particular solution to get a job done; it should include those who hire varying solutions. Furthermore, the customer group should be defined by responsibility area rather than by job title or by demographic (for example, age or income) or firmographic (for example, company size or industry) characteristics. And customers who are responsible *exclusively* for consumption chain jobs, such as deciding upon a vendor or paying for a service, should not be the innovation focus unless the goal is supplementary service innovation.

Finally, the company must decide upon the scope of investigation. This means defining the core job if the company is going to pursue core service innovation or deciding on what scope of jobs to uncover for new service innovation. (These topics are covered in depth in the chapters on each of the innovation approaches.) The important thing to remember is that you can't have an infinitely broad scope, either in terms of jobs or customer groups, to study. The same factors a company takes into account when prioritizing its product portfolio (alignment with strategy, revenue potential, ability to lead the market, and so on) apply when prioritizing jobs or customer groups for the innovation effort.

Step 2. Uncover Customer Needs

Once the innovation focus is defined, the next step is to uncover customer needs—but we are looking at their needs in terms of the jobs they are trying to get done and the outcomes they are hoping to achieve, not in terms of particular service features or ideas. For the task of capturing customer needs, we rely on a combination of one-on-one interviews, small group interviews, and observational interviews.

Now perhaps you've read in other business advice books that it's a waste of time to turn to customers for information on their needs. Some so-called experts say customers do not know what they need and cannot articulate those needs even if they know what they are. But those experts are wrong. When your focus is on the job rather than on the solution, customers are the most reliable sources of information.[2] Subsequent chapters will explain what questions to ask to uncover job- and outcome-related customer needs. For now, it's enough to remind yourself to focus on the job that the customer is trying to get done and the needs that the customer has that arise from trying to get the job done.

The number of people you should interview to understand customer needs depends on the scope of the investigation, but generally speaking, 15 interviews (plus or minus) will provide a thorough understanding for any of the service innovation options. (Note that a group interview counts as only one interview, even if there are six customers in the group.) Fifteen interviews should allow you to capture 80 to 100 high-quality customer needs, depending upon your innovation focus. These needs will be expressed as either job statements (which describe the jobs the customer is trying to get done) or as outcome statements (which describe the outcomes the customer desires in doing a given job).

A trained interviewer can capture 20 to 30 high-quality job or outcome statements in a single one-hour customer interview. We find it very useful to talk to as diverse a group of customers as possible (that is, varying ages, income levels, industries, firm sizes, experience levels, and so on) to ensure that all needs are captured for the scope of the study in as few interviews as possible.

Jobs

A job defines the action for which a service is hired or may be hired. These actions consist of either goals that customers want to accomplish or problems they are trying to avoid or resolve. Examples of goals for which services are hired include invest for retirement (Charles Schwab), send a package (FedEx), and purchase a book (Amazon.com). Examples of problems (to avoid or resolve) for which services are hired include prevent a home burglary (ADT), correct poor vision (LASIK eye surgery), and rid a home of termites (Terminix).

A job statement always follows the structure shown in Figure 1-3.[3] Because a job specifies the action for which a service might be hired, a job statement always includes an action verb followed by a specific object of action (for example, *learn to play guitar, buy a home, find someone to marry*).

Optionally, a job statement may contain a contextual clarifier to describe the conditions or circumstances under which the

**Figure 1-3   The Structure of a Customer
Job Statement**

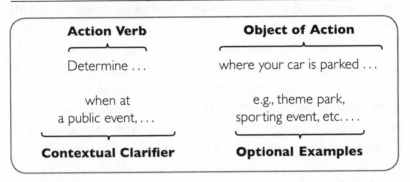

job is executed (for example, *get a prescription filled **when ill,**
stay overnight **while traveling with family***). It may also contain
examples to further clarify the object of action. When one specific context is specified, other relevant contexts of job execution should also be considered.

In order to be an effective guide to service innovation, a job
must reflect what the customer is really trying to accomplish,
be relevant across individuals in the customer group (for
example, across genders, ages, or geography), be stable over
time, and be specific enough to prompt an unambiguous course
of action. To articulate a job that meets these requirements, a
job statement must comply with certain rules. In particular, a
good job statement must not include any references to how the
need might be satisfied—it should not mention solutions, technologies, services, and so on. Thus, *get insight from an MRI* is
not a good job statement if your innovation focus is health
diagnosis. Better would be job statements such as *determine if
one has a broken bone* or *determine the cause of lower back pain.*

In addition, a good job statement must reflect what the customers are really trying to accomplish, not just a task to get
them there. So, for example, when considering customers' per-

sonal health jobs, exercise is merely a task to help customers to *lose weight, build muscle tone,* and *maintain flexibility.* Finally, a good job statement must use unambiguous language so that all who read it will understand it in the same way—including customers and internal stakeholders. Thus, imprecise words such as *usable, dependable,* and *effectively* must be avoided. Such imprecision introduces variation in interpretation that hampers innovation. Ultimately, the statement must provide the detail required to guide the innovation process without constraining innovation to a particular solution.

Desired Outcomes

An outcome is a metric that customers use to define the successful execution of a job. Thus, outcomes are nested under jobs. A simple job may have only a handful of outcomes. However, a complex job may involve a dozen or more steps and 100 to 150 outcomes.

An outcome statement always follows the structure shown in Figure 1-4. Because an outcome is a measure of success, it includes a direction of improvement, a unit of measure, and a very specific object of control that defines what is being mea-

Figure 1-4   The Structure of a Customer Outcome Statement

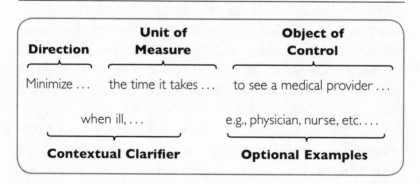

sured by the customer. As with job statements, an outcome statement may contain a contextual clarifier to describe the conditions or circumstances under which the measurement is relevant (for example, *increase the likelihood of getting a diagnosis during the office visit*) and examples to further clarify the object of control. To avoid introducing unnecessary variability into outcome statements, we use only *minimize* or *increase* for direction. In fact, because customers most often measure success by reduced time, variability, and deviations from the ideal output, most outcomes reflect the customers' desire to minimize something. Among the many units of measure available, the majority of outcomes rely on a few basic measurements, including time, likelihood, number, amount, and frequency.

To articulate an outcome effectively, an outcome statement, like a job statement, must not suggest solutions, must be specific to what the customer is really trying to control, and must be unambiguous. It must also, of course, truly be a measure of success in accomplishing some step in getting a particular job done. The resulting statement may sound rather distant from a customer's casual remark, but in fact it is not. For example, in describing steps in the job of conducting an Internet search, a customer might say, "I wish I didn't have to sort through so much irrelevant information." This means that one way this customer measures success in conducting an Internet search is by how much irrelevant information he or she has to sort through—the less, the better. Expressing the customer's desired outcome in the format of an outcome statement gives us *minimize the amount of irrelevant information returned by a search query*. Though not the customer's exact words, the statement does reflect one of the customer's measures of success. As part of the innovation process, we read both job and outcome statements back to customers during their interviews to verify that the wording captures what they are trying to achieve.

Step 3. Prioritize Customer Needs

After determining the customer's needs, the next step is prioritization. All customer needs are not created equal—not in the eyes of the customer, and not from an innovation perspective. A company wants to focus its time and resources on those customer needs that are very important to customers but are not well satisfied by today's solutions.[4] Those needs represent the best opportunities for service innovation.

To prioritize customer needs, we survey a representative sample of customers and have them rate the needs on two criteria: importance and satisfaction. Specifically, for each job and/or outcome statement, we ask customers to rate importance on a five-point scale from "not important at all" to "extremely important," following the lead-in, "How important is it to you that you are able to . . . ?" Customers also rate satisfaction on a five-point scale, from "not satisfied at all" to "extremely satisfied," following the lead-in, "How satisfied are you with your ability to . . . ?" or "How satisfied are you that current solutions enable you to . . . ?" If customer jobs are what the company is investigating, then customers will rate job statements. If a specific job is the focus, then customers will rate outcome statements for steps in getting the job done. Sometimes, in a particular investigation, a company may uncover both outcomes on a job and new or related jobs, in which case customers will be rating both jobs and outcomes.

The customer needs that represent the best opportunities for service innovation are those that are important but not well satisfied. Therefore, we use a simple algorithm to combine importance and satisfaction ratings and provide a single number with which to rank the needs. The opportunity algorithm, shown in Figure 1-5, states that opportunity equals importance plus the difference between importance and satisfaction.[5]

Any opportunity score over 10 represents a promising opportunity. Thus, if 85 percent of customers rate a particular

Figure 1-5   The Opportunity Algorithm

Opportunity = importance + *max* (importance − satisfaction, 0)

---

job as very important or extremely important (the top two importance options on the five-point scale) and only 45 percent of customers say that they are very satisfied or extremely satisfied (the top two satisfaction options on the five-point scale) with their ability to get the job done, then the opportunity score for this job is 8.5 + (8.5 − 4.5), which equals 12.5—a very solid opportunity indeed.[6] Customer jobs or outcomes with higher opportunity scores are those for which customers will most value service innovation.

Opportunity scores can also be compared for different subgroups of customers in the survey to identify opportunities that are unique to each. For example, if some customers use Brand A to get the job done and some customers use Brand B to get the same job done, then you can compare the level of opportunity for one brand to the other. The same holds true for other groups of customers included in the survey such as large firms versus small firms, men versus women, and so on. Finally, a company should also consider whether it would be insightful to have some customers rate the outcomes for one context in which the job is executed and other customers rate the same outcomes for a different context to see if distinct contexts present unique opportunities. (For example, how does a teacher's job of creating an assignment *for a class* compare with the outcome priorities if the assignment is created *for an individual*? Or how do the struggles in doing the job of managing cash flow *when one is employed* differ from those when doing the same job *when one has lost a job*?)

Critics occasionally like to nitpick at the details of the prioritization process. They may prefer seven-point scales or three-point scales to five-point scales, or they may believe you should use the mean rather than the top two options on the five-point scale, or they may have some other quibble. Don't let those criticisms distract you. What's important is to focus on jobs and outcomes, and to prioritize *all* the jobs and outcomes you have uncovered based on importance and satisfaction. Customer needs that are very important but not well satisfied represent good opportunities for innovation.

Step 4. Develop a Service Strategy

The final step in the innovation process is to use the high-opportunity customer needs obtained from the prioritization process to guide the development of a successful service strategy—that is, a service strategy that puts the company in the position of offering a unique and valuable service (or services) to customers. An effective service strategy spells out who the target customer is, what customer needs the service satisfies, and what the important elements of the service concept are. The service concept describes (1) the important elements of the service design from a marketing, human resources, operations, and IT perspective and (2) the important elements of the service delivery system, including the role that people, equipment, procedures, and the physical facility play in satisfying customer needs.[7] It's at this stage of the innovation process that the unique nature of services must be addressed, along with the roles that marketing, human resources, operations, and IT will play in defining and delivering the value customers are seeking. We will cover those aspects of the process in depth in Chapters 6 to 8.

In devising breakthrough services, companies will also have to take into account how well their capabilities, resources, culture, and strategy align with what it would take to deliver on the customer need opportunities. A successful service strategy weds what the customer will value with what the company can deliver. However, a company must also be willing to expand its capabilities—whether by internal development, acquisition, or partnerships—when the right opportunities present themselves. Once the company has come up with a service concept that aligns with its capabilities, resources, and strategy, the next step is the actual design and development of the service.

SUMMARY

The secret to successful service innovation is understanding how customers define value. Customers hire products and services to help them get jobs done, and they measure their success in getting those jobs done by how well they are able to achieve certain desired outcomes. Customers' opinions of a service are also influenced by their experience "consuming" the service. When we consider what job the customer is trying to get done and what the customer must do to consume particular solutions that help with getting the job done, we arrive at four possible approaches to service innovation—core service innovation, new service innovation, service delivery innovation, and supplementary service innovation.

To go from innovation objectives to a service strategy built around a unique and valuable service concept, a company must (1) select the innovation focus, (2) uncover customer needs, (3) prioritize customer needs, and (4) develop a service strategy. More specifically, a company must define the customer and the type and scope of needs to uncover, talk to customers to understand the jobs and outcomes they are trying to achieve, get a representative sample of customers to rate the importance and satisfaction of those jobs and outcomes, thereby revealing the best opportunities for innovation, and spell out the important service design and delivery system elements that are going to enable the company to provide customers with a valuable service solution that is differentiated from, and superior to, those offered by competitors.

CHAPTER 2

DISCOVER OPPORTUNITIES FOR NEW SERVICE INNOVATION

Customers hire services to help them accomplish the many jobs they need to get done. Any given customer—whether a consumer or a business client—has many jobs to be done. Once the job is accepted as the unit of analysis, the goal of innovation changes. The primary goal of service innovation is no longer to innovate service. Rather, the primary goal is to help customers get a specific job done better or to help them get more jobs done. It is only a secondary goal to provide an essentially intangible service to help customers in this way.

Apple understands the benefits of helping customers get more jobs done: Through iTunes, the iPhone, and an open development environment, Apple is reaping the financial rewards of helping consumers and professionals get many, many jobs done better. Take the apps for the iPhone. Although many of the apps target leisure time (which is appropriate: overcoming boredom and being challenged mentally are also, by our definition, jobs that customers would like to get done), there are also many apps that are tied to more serious, and often very specific, jobs. Among the top 25 apps at the time of this writing, for example, are Offender Locator (which helps customers find out if registered sex offenders live in the area), Lyrics+ (which helps customers find the lyrics to a song), iFitness (which helps customers find new exercise routines), CameraZoom (which lets customers take a zoom photo with the iPhone), and ColorSplash (which lets customers enhance photos). And requests for medical, education, and business apps are up dramatically. As Apple seeks to penetrate the business professional market, its best bet is to develop a comprehensive understanding of the jobs that busy professionals need or want to get done while on the go. These might include, for example, determining the status of a work project, staying up-to-date on new competitive offerings, or finding evidence to support a case.

This chapter explains how a company can discover *new* service innovation opportunities by uncovering more jobs that the customer wants to get done. Many companies struggle with this element of service innovation: they are unsure what customer jobs to satisfy with new services. We will consider multiple approaches to uncovering these jobs. Once a list of jobs is uncovered, the company should proceed with prioritizing them, as described in Chapter 1, to determine which jobs represent opportunities for innovation. With a list of these innovation opportunities in hand, the company will be well positioned to move to the concept creation phase. Let's consider some methods of discovering the jobs for which new services might be offered.

Discover Why Your Service Is Hired

Many services are hired by the customer to get many jobs done. Investors hire a financial advisor, for example, to develop a financial plan that enables them to achieve a variety of family, education, and retirement jobs that rely on finances. In the same way, students take classes to learn about many different topics and to develop a variety of different career skills. The best starting point for new service innovation, therefore, is to figure out the jobs for which the company's services are already being hired.

Recently, we worked with a manufacturer of LASIK equipment in which we asked LASIK techs the reasons why they contacted vendor support or relied on vendor support materials. We asked about clinical decisions they were trying to make, clinical problems they were trying to resolve, and other jobs that benefitted from vendor service and support. Taking this approach, we uncovered more than 50 distinct jobs for which LASIK vendor support was already being hired. The jobs spanned a wide range of clinical responsibilities, including patient counseling (for example, *educate a patient about available treatment options*); procedure planning (for example, *find out the range of approved treatment parameters for the laser*); postoperative care (for example, *get a patient to comply with postop guidelines*); and working with a laser (for example, *understand how the laser has changed following an upgrade*). Although the basis for uncovering these jobs was current support contacts, any one of them could have been the basis for stand-alone new services to create further value for the techs.

We conducted a similar study for a leading provider of online science information that was interested in knowing the jobs for which its services were being hired. We interviewed research scientists to uncover the jobs they were trying to get done when searching for scientific information. What information were they trying to find? What decisions were they trying to make? From only a half-dozen personal interviews and a couple of small group interviews, we identified over 100 jobs. We discovered that at the most basic level, research scientists rely on electronic searches to help with jobs related to understanding, such as keeping current in a research area and determining what causes something. At an intermediate level, research scientists rely on electronic searches to help with jobs related to guidance, such as determining how to explain a finding or determining what actions others have taken in a situation. At the highest level, research scientists rely on electronic searches to help with jobs related to discovery and explanation, such as devising a hypothesis to advance a theory or determining the reason for an empirical result. As with the LASIK equipment manufacturer, any one of these jobs or a group of related jobs could provide the basis for new or improved services.

As these examples illustrate, a company can uncover the jobs for which current services are hired by asking a few simple questions that tie back to the definition of a job. Customers should be asked these questions:

- What are you trying to accomplish by using this service?
- What goals or objectives does this service help you to accomplish?
- What problems does this service help you to prevent or resolve?

It may also be valuable to uncover jobs related to distinct contexts in which a service is hired (where, when, with whom)—for example, at home or away from home; alone or with children. A restaurant taking this approach might find that customers hire food service when hosting a birthday celebration, having an intimate picnic in the park, hosting a formal dinner at home, having a meal while traveling in a car, or having a meal with children, among many other context-based jobs. Of course, the questioner must be willing to probe a bit further to ensure that the jobs that are uncovered meet the criteria for a good job statement, but in general, you can obtain much rich insight with these simple questions.

Discover Why Your Service Might Be Hired

With a simple change in the frame of reference, a company can also uncover the jobs for which current or new services *might* be hired. To accomplish this, questions should focus the customers on what the ideal service would help them to accomplish. It is amazing how much this change of perspective helps with eliciting new jobs—even with very professional audiences. When I asked the LASIK technicians to tell me what the ideal vendor service or support would help them to accomplish, I learned about such jobs as determining the patient's expectations for outcomes following treatment, alleviating patient anxiety during the procedure, and understanding possible causes of a clinical complication. These were jobs that the laser vendor was not currently targeting, and yet they were closely related to its current services.

Another useful approach is to uncover the jobs that customers are trying to get done (or would like to get done) before, during, and after hiring the company's current service. This approach is very effective at uncovering jobs that customers are trying to get done that are very closely related to current services. This might lead to new offerings as part of a current service or entirely new services. For example, if a mobile service provider asked customers what other tasks they do while on a call that relate to the call itself, answers would include things such as scribbling notes and checking calendars. Scribbling notes, of course, is itself a solution that the customer may be using to get a number of jobs done. With a few follow-up questions, the mobile company would discover that the jobs customers are trying to get done by scribbling notes include capturing the important points of a call, sharing the key points of a call with others, making changes to a calendar based on a call, and creating a personal to-do list based on a call—any one of which could be the basis for new or improved services that the mobile service provider might offer.[1]

To uncover jobs for which your service might be hired, ask customers these questions:

- What would the ideal service help you to accomplish?
- What else are you trying to accomplish before, during, or after using the current service?
- What other responsibilities do you have before, during, or after using the current service?
- What other services would you like to be offered before, during, or after using the current service? What would each allow you to accomplish?

This is the approach that Microsoft took to discover service innovation opportunities for Software Assurance, its software maintenance offering. Until 2004, Microsoft viewed Software Assurance simply as a vehicle for the efficient purchase of software upgrades. In exchange for a flat fee, corporate customers who signed a multiyear contract received operating system upgrade rights. However, with renewal rates declining, Microsoft decided to reconsider the needs that Software Assurance might satisfy. Rather than maintaining a strict focus on helping with the purchase of a software license, Microsoft sought to discover what other jobs Software Assurance might help the customer get done.

To do so, Microsoft interviewed 30 IT decision makers and 20 IT professionals who manage software deployment about the other responsibilities that they had related to managing and supporting software before, during, and after the purchase or renewal of a software license. From these interviews, Microsoft uncovered 34 jobs of IT decision makers and 61 jobs of IT professionals. IT decision makers reported that they needed to accomplish the following:

- Determine software license costs for the next budget year
- Ensure compliance with existing license arrangements

IT professionals reported that they needed to meet these responsibilities:

- Train users on basic software functionality
- Determine if users have unlicensed copies of software
- Determine if new software is compatible with existing applications
- Determine the optimal rollout procedure for deploying new software

By taking a look at the complete suite of jobs that IT decision makers and professionals needed to get done, Microsoft realized that it was really engaging with customers for only one tiny piece of their overall responsibilities. Following a prioritization of the jobs for importance and satisfaction, Microsoft adopted a life cycle management view of the business, and it introduced many new products and services to the Software Assurance offering that aligned with this perspective. For example, Microsoft discovered that customers were having trouble tracking software inventory and the number of licenses in use. To help them get these jobs done better, Microsoft introduced an online asset inventory service that made it possible to maintain accurate information about all the software installed on desktops throughout the organization. This service also provided the IT decision maker with the insight needed to forecast software needs with confidence. To address customer jobs related to software deployment and upgrades, Microsoft instituted a program of training vouchers that gave IT professionals access to certified Microsoft trainers. Microsoft also added deployment consulting services to help IT professionals create comprehensive deployment plans. In the year

Microsoft announced these and other changes to Software Assurance, it beat its revenue goal by over 10 percent, and renewal rates and revenue have continued to grow ever since.

Discover Other Jobs of Customers

It is also possible—and highly productive—to uncover jobs for which new services might be hired by starting with the customer rather than the service. In this case, the company identifies a customer group—whether one that it already serves or not—and decides what type of jobs it wants to uncover using a word or two descriptor (for example, *innovation jobs, personal finance jobs*) or a brief phrase to describe an area of customer responsibility (for example, *jobs related to running a small business, jobs related to caring for an aging parent*).

To uncover the specific customer jobs in this broader area of responsibility, it is not necessary or even desirable to tie the questions back to current services. Rather, customers are asked these questions:

- What are you trying to accomplish in this job area? What tasks and/or activities?
- What are your goals and objectives?
- What problems are you trying to prevent or resolve?
- What are you trying to determine or decide?

Microsoft HealthVault, for example, has taken this approach to discover new service innovation opportunities for different customer groups it serves. HealthVault helps consumers, for example, with personal health and wellness jobs in five distinct job categories: losing or maintaining weight, getting and staying fit, managing high blood pressure, organizing family health information, and preparing for an emergency. "What do you want to do?" the HealthVault Web site asks, and customers can then choose from among those five topics. Under each topic, HealthVault offers a variety of Web applications and information about other recommended health devices. And this is just the beginning. HealthVault executives are currently exploring other health and wellness jobs that consumers are struggling to get done.

When taking this approach, the customer group should be defined as broadly as possible. In particular, it should not be limited to the company's customers or even to the customers of a particular product or service. Rather, the customer group should be defined broadly to include any individuals who have responsibilities in the job area of interest and who might be of interest for the company to serve (for example, small business owners or adults with an elderly parent).[2]

In looking at the types of customer jobs to investigate, a company should direct its attention toward ones that it would be willing to target with services. That decision will be based on company strategy, specific innovation objectives, and capabilities and resources. The home insurance company Chubb, for example, targets the other jobs that owners of high-end custom homes are trying to get done related to *protecting the value of home assets*. Chubb helps its customers get other jobs done in this area with its collector services—services that help homeowners make better decisions regarding personal collections—and with its Masterpiece HomeScan Service that helps homeowners identify the location of problems needing repairs and hidden building defects.

The overarching job area that a company targets should be broad enough to encompass a variety of specific jobs. Consider a general area of customer responsibility that relates to current services offered by the company. Typically, this is going to be a higher-level abstraction of the specific jobs for which any given current service might be hired. For example, if the company currently helps customers perform the job of purchasing pet food and supplies, as was the case with PetSmart, then a broad area in which jobs might be captured is caring for a pet.[3] A search in that area would reveal many jobs that the company could target with services.

In addition, if the company can identify subcategories of jobs that might be captured—job responsibility areas, if you will—the discovery process will be even more productive. If the company doesn't know these in advance, however, it's not a problem: commonalities among jobs will emerge during the first few customer interviews. For example, if my initial interviews with pet owners indicate that the jobs they are trying to get done include getting a sick pet to eat, keeping a pet from jumping on furniture, and ridding a pet of fleas, then I can reasonably begin to create categories to guide my subsequent interviews. These might include caring for a sick pet, pet behavior challenges, and pet health and wellness issues.

I also strongly recommend that companies consider the types of *actions* their services might be hired to help with. That is, anticipate the specific verbs that might characterize the jobs that customers are trying to get done. If I am in a medical space, for example, I should anticipate hearing many jobs that begin with *prevent, relieve,* and *maintain.* If I am in an educational space, I should anticipate many jobs that begin with *learn, develop,* and *determine.* If I am investigating insurance, I should anticipate many jobs that begin with *protect, cover,* and *ensure*—and so on. Once you know some of the verbs that make sense in a context, whether because you anticipated them beforehand or recognized them once you started hearing them from customers, then you can use those actions to help uncover more jobs. What other conditions are you trying to relieve? What else are you trying to ensure? What other things are you trying to learn? Table 2-1 provides a list of common verbs for jobs that my colleagues and I have encountered.

Consider how the Society for Human Resource Management (SHRM) followed this approach to new service innovation. SHRM is a membership organization focused on advancing the human resource profession, so its managers focused on discovering the various jobs that senior HR professionals struggle to get done. The management team guiding the investigation asked HR professionals to describe the jobs they were trying to get done in 24 different responsibility areas, including recruiting, training, performance management, compensation and benefits, legal compliance, and organizational culture. In each area, the SHRM team asked about the tasks the HR professionals were trying to get done, the goals they were trying to accomplish, and the problems they were trying to resolve.

When HR professionals mentioned solutions such as benchmarking competitive executive salaries, a trained interviewer was sure to ask a follow-up question to uncover the job the solution helped the professional get done—in that case, *ensuring that jobs are priced competitively in a given market.* A combination of personal and group interviews with 38 HR professionals

Table 2-1   Common Verbs for Customer Jobs

Achieve	Discover	Learn	Relieve
Allow	Ensure	Locate	Remember
Confirm	Experience	Maintain	Remove
Coordinate	Find	Make	Share
Correct	Fix	Obtain	Stay
Create	Get	Plan	Stop
Demonstrate	Help	Prepare	Teach
Detect	Identify	Prevent	Understand
Determine	Improve	Protect	Update
Develop	Keep	Provide	Verify

helped SHRM to uncover 195 different jobs. SHRM followed the interviews up with a survey in which over 400 HR professionals rated the importance of the jobs and their satisfaction with their ability to accomplish them, resulting in a list of opportunities for SHRM to address with new training programs, new conference sessions, new ways to partner with corporations, and other services.

In practice, the jobs for which current services are or might be hired and the other jobs of customers are not mutually exclusive; on the contrary, they may have considerable overlap. However, looking at the task of developing new services from multiple angles provides a company with alternative ways to think about uncovering more jobs. Table 2-2 provides examples of studies my colleagues and I have undertaken in several service industries to uncover customer jobs.

Discover Experience Jobs of Customers

There is also a special class of jobs for which services might be hired—experiences.[4] People may want to experience competition, nature, a physical challenge, or a historical time period. Some services are primarily hired for the experience they provide—theme parks and theaters, for example. Even services that are intended primarily to help people resolve problems can also be hired to accomplish an experience-oriented job. People hire restaurants, for example, to obtain a meal without the hassle of food preparation, but they may also hire a restaurant to experience authentic cuisine from a foreign culture. Similarly, people may hire a particular retail venue to experience the thrill of finding a bargain or to enjoy camaraderie with friends.

The point in calling special attention to experience jobs is to ensure that their potential for innovation won't be overlooked—

Table 2-2 Examples of New Service Innovation Studies

Industry	Customer	Job Area	Job Examples
Construction	Job site supervisor	Managing construction	• Find qualified workers • Confirm the availability of required construction materials
Education	Teacher	Teaching role	• Create a course syllabus • Create exercises to develop a specific skill
Financial services	Consumer	Money management	• Control impulse spending • Pay for an online purchase
Health care	Consumer	Personal health	• Diagnose the cause of an illness • Prevent an unwanted pregnancy
Hospitality	Consumer	Restroom uses	• Remove a stain from clothing • Discipline a child
Insurance	Benefits manager	Plan management	• Enroll new hires in a health plan • Determine how benefit use compares to prior years

(continued)

Table 2-2 Examples of New Service Innovation Studies (continued)

Industry	Customer	Job Area	Job Examples
Personal services	Consumer	Local search	• Find contact information for a business • Determine what menu items are offered at a restaurant
Professional services	Human resources director	Employee management	• Verify the background of potential hires • Develop a compensation structure for the organization
Retail	Consumer	Online shopping	• Find a product to replace one that has broken • Learn about trends in a purchase category
Utilities	Building manager	Energy management	• Prevent an interruption in energy supply • Identify energy inefficiencies in a building

especially for those services in which the experience is the reason for the service. However, it does not mean that a distinct approach is required to uncover or prioritize them. In fact, a company can take the same approach to uncovering experience jobs as other types of jobs—talk to customers.

Consider the case of the social networking service Facebook. In just five years, Facebook has risen from nothing to over 350 million active users. Its popularity draws from the unique social experience it offers users. But does that mean that users cannot articulate why they hire Facebook? Does it mean that we cannot discover other jobs that users might like to get done? Not at all. In fact, the main reasons why Facebook is hired are easy to articulate and can be readily uncovered by asking users to discuss the reasons for their activities and posts. Among other jobs, Facebook users are trying to connect with old friends, get to know friends better, share the details of their lives with others, let others know how they are feeling, find help for a problem, support a cause, meet people with common interests, inspire others to support a cause, learn about what others think about a topic, encourage others who are down, share about a good or bad experience, stay connected with others during the day, share interesting personal information, let others know they care, and, of course, overcome boredom at work.

When seeking to uncover experience jobs, customers should be asked the same questions that are used to elicit other jobs. However, you should expect to hear some distinct verbs when experience jobs are being uncovered. Some of the more common verbs associated with experience jobs are *experience, discover, appreciate, learn, inspire, escape, enjoy, be* or *become, achieve, support, share, remember,* and even *forget.* With these in mind, a few questions designed specifically to elicit experience jobs should also be asked. These include the following:

- What experiences are you seeking?
- What are you trying to experience, discover, appreciate, and so on, by using this service?
- What would the ideal solution help you to experience, discover, appreciate, and so on?

Finally, it will also be useful to anticipate possible categories of experiences, such as those related to education, escape, entertainment, and aesthetics.[5] For example, we did a study to uncover life experience jobs of teens that focused on such job categories as discovering who you are, expressing who you are, growing as a person, improving mental outlook, understanding the world, reflecting on life, connecting with others, helping others, supporting a cause, and building relationships.

Discover Emotional Jobs

Most of the time, when we think of jobs, we think of tasks that need to be done, but sometimes customers hire products and services for more than the functions they provide. Sometimes they hire them for the emotional needs they satisfy. These emotional needs are jobs, and many services require a focus on emotional jobs. This is certainly true for services such as counseling, health care, hospitality, and a variety of personal services such as spas and child care providers. It is also true, however, for services with seemingly little focus on the emotional needs of customers. FedEx advertising, for example, often appeals to the emotional jobs of its customers such as the need to avoid feeling anxious, feel important, and be perceived as competent.

There are two types of emotional jobs: the emotional jobs that deal with what a person wants to feel or avoid feeling (feel loved, feel confident, avoid feeling guilty, and so on), and the emotional jobs that deal with how a person wants to be perceived or avoid being perceived (be perceived as intelligent, be perceived as a good parent, avoid being perceived as unprofessional, and so on). These jobs are different from functional jobs that have an emotional component, such as overcoming depression, finding someone to marry, or relieving stress. It is important to be clear on the distinction because the customer ultimately defines value for functional jobs based on how well the function is delivered—even when the job has a strong emotional component. With emotional jobs, by comparison, the customer defines value by how well the emotional need is satisfied. The easiest way to tell the two types of jobs apart is by looking at the verb: all emotional job statements start with *feel*, *avoid feeling*, *be perceived as*, or *avoid being perceived as*. If the job statement doesn't start with those words, then the job is not an emotional job.

Some emotional jobs relate to life in general (feel loved, feel significant, feel secure); others relate to specific services[6] or functional jobs. Microsoft's Software Assurance, discussed earlier, provides a good example of the latter. In interviewing IT professionals, Microsoft discovered that in addition to their many functional jobs, the professionals had certain emotional jobs as well, which revolved around being perceived as adding value to their organizations. These professionals were tired of being viewed as a cost center; they were looking for ways to be perceived differently. To address this opportunity, Microsoft hired Gartner, a leading IT research and advisory firm, to put together an objective return-on-investment (ROI) toolkit that would demonstrate the value of purchasing a Software Assurance agreement in terms of time savings, cost savings, and so on. The ROI toolkit enabled the IT professionals to demonstrate the wisdom of their decision to purchase Software Assurance—helping them to accomplish the emotional job of being perceived as adding value to their organization—and it is now a part of the standard sales engagement.

For most companies, it will make more sense to uncover the emotional jobs associated with a particular functional job or job area. My favorite way of eliciting these emotional jobs is to ask, "If you had the ideal solution for getting this job done (or for getting jobs done in this job area), how would that make you feel, or how would you be perceived? What feelings or perceptions would be avoided?" When I asked these questions of financial services customers in the context of the functional job area of managing personal finances, they told me that they wanted to feel worry free, feel secure, avoid feeling guilty, and be perceived as responsible. In response to those emotional jobs, financial institutions can offer services such as overdraft protection and automatic bill payment, which not only satisfy functional needs related to managing cash flow but also help customers accomplish the emotional jobs of feeling secure and being perceived as responsible.

Service innovation ultimately depends on understanding both the functional and emotional jobs that the customer is trying to get done. Functional jobs are the primary basis for innovation of the inner workings of a service—what the service does, what is delivered to the customer, how a service operates, the technical skills of employees, and the service's technological capabilities. Emotional jobs, in contrast, are the primary basis for positioning, messaging, and managing the physical clues of service delivery (for example, the look and feel of the physical environment, personnel, materials). And both functional and emotional jobs provide the foundation for designing a service to both deliver function and impact the customer experience (for example, service policies, layout, pricing structure).

Discover New and Emerging Jobs

Jobs are very stable over time. Just consider the many different jobs that have been mentioned in this chapter. Ask yourself: Were customers trying to get this job done 20 years ago? Will customers be getting this job done 20 years from now? I would venture to say that in nearly all cases, the answer to both questions will be an unequivocal yes. Sure, the solutions change, and even how the job is executed changes. But, in most cases, the job endures for decades. In *most* cases. Although jobs are very stable over time, new jobs do emerge, and a company should always be on the lookout for these new jobs for which new services might be hired.

There are three primary reasons why new jobs emerge: advances in knowledge; changes in laws, policies, or regulations; and new solutions or technologies.

- *Advances in knowledge.* First, new jobs emerge with advances in human knowledge. In the decades following the discovery of DNA and related scientific insights, for example, many new jobs emerged, including sequencing a full genome, synthesizing a new protein, and predicting disease based on individual genetics.
- *Changes in laws, policies, or regulations.* Second, new jobs may emerge due to changes in laws, policies, or regulations—sometimes laws that are enacted to deal with new scientific discoveries, as in the case of laws concerning privacy of health information. Laws designed to protect the environment, for example, have created a number of new jobs relating to reducing pollution from manufacturing operations, implementing an environmental compliance program when building a home, and designing a water-conserving landscape.

- *New solutions or technologies.* Finally, new jobs often emerge as new solutions and technologies are adopted. With the invention of computers and software, for example, came such new jobs as developing software, recovering lost data, and protecting a computer from external threats. And to support these new jobs have come a variety of new services, including software development services, data recovery services, and Internet security services.

To anticipate the emergence of jobs for which new services might be offered, a company must track knowledge discoveries, legal and regulatory changes, and technology developments related to its industry or core competency areas with one question in mind: what new jobs will emerge as a result? Company insiders who already know the industry well can be very adept at answering this question once they have a clear understanding of how a job is defined.

"What new actions or tasks will a business or consumer need to accomplish as a result of a particular knowledge discovery, legal or regulatory change, or technology development?" This question can be posed to a panel of industry experts or even leading-edge customers, who can also provide insight into relevant discoveries, laws, and innovations likely to affect the industry. Many companies already have customer advisory boards and key opinion leaders to whom they can turn with this question.

There is a fourth area that companies should also track in order to anticipate new service innovation possibilities—trends. With trends, a new job has probably not emerged, but trends do affect which jobs are considered significant, and that's important because as a job becomes more significant, customers' interest in it and need to accomplish it are likely to increase. Companies must be vigilant about monitoring trends in the customer, natural, sociocultural, economic, business, and political and legal environments with the goal of determining how key trends are likely to affect the significance of different customer jobs.

Because trends simply reflect trajectories over time, some customers are already dealing with the issues impacted by the trend. As such, a company can benefit by discovering the job priorities of customers who are at the leading edge of the trend. For example, one key customer trend in much of the world is that the population is aging. If a company wants to anticipate the jobs for which new services might be created as the population ages, it should seek to discover the high-priority jobs of today's elderly—especially any jobs that are specifically tied to aging or that are particularly challenging due to aging. For example, a company could uncover the jobs that the elderly must accomplish to enable them to age in place. This would include jobs that could benefit from new services such as retrofitting a bathroom, monitoring a medical condition, and protecting a home from intruders.

SUMMARY

Once the job is accepted as the focus of service innovation, the logical conclusion is that a company's innovation of new services should be guided by an understanding of the jobs that customers are trying to get done. Table 2-3 summarizes the approaches to uncovering jobs presented in this chapter.

To uncover the jobs for which current services are being hired or might be hired, a company can ask customers what they are trying to accomplish by using a particular service, what the ideal service would help them accomplish, what else they are trying to get done before, during, and after using the service, and what goals they have and problems they are trying to resolve in a particular area of responsibility.

(continued)

Table 2-3   Approaches to Discovering Customer Jobs

Approach	Questions to Consider
Discover why current services are being hired	• What are you trying to accomplish by using this service? • What goals or objectives does this service help you to accomplish? • What problems does this service help you to prevent or resolve?
Discover why current services might be hired	• What would the ideal service help you to accomplish? • What else are you trying to accomplish before, during, or after using the current service? • What other responsibilities do you have before, during, or after using the current service? • What other services would you like to be offered before, during, or after using the current service? What would each allow you to accomplish?
Discover other customer jobs (in an area of responsibility)	• What are you trying to accomplish in this job area? What tasks and/or activities? • In this job area, what are your goals and objectives? • In this job area, what problems are you trying to prevent or resolve? • In this job area, what are you trying to determine or decide?
Discover experience jobs	• What experiences are you seeking? • What are you trying to experience by using this service? • What would the ideal solution help you to experience?

Discover emotional jobs	• If you had the ideal solution for getting this job done (or in this job area), how would that make you feel, or how would you be perceived? What feelings or perceptions would be avoided?
Discover new and emerging customer jobs	• What new jobs will a customer need to accomplish as a result of a particular knowledge discovery, legal or regulatory change, or technology development?

Companies should also be aware that sometimes acquiring a certain experience can be a job and that services are not only hired for the functions they deliver but also for the emotional jobs they satisfy. Finally, a company should always be on the lookout for new or emerging jobs derived from advances in knowledge, legal or regulatory changes, new solutions and technologies, and various trends.

The methods presented in this chapter provide a comprehensive approach to uncovering customer jobs to drive new service innovation. With a basic understanding of what a job is and the guidance provided in this chapter, any company can begin to identify the jobs for which it might create new services. Once it knows which of these jobs holds the most opportunity—those that are important but not well satisfied by today's solutions—it will know exactly where to focus its service innovation efforts.

CHAPTER 3

DISCOVER OPPORTUNITIES FOR CORE SERVICE INNOVATION

The goal of core service innovation is to help customers get a particular job done better. It begins by asking the question, "What core job is the customer trying to accomplish by hiring this service (or these complementary services)?" Once the job is known, the company must learn what steps the customer must take in order to complete the job successfully. At each of those steps, there are potential innovation opportunities. Though the starting point for core service innovation is often one or more current service offerings, the true anchor for core service innovation is the job the customer is trying to get done, which means that core service innovation may result in improvements or extensions to current services, but it can also lead to entirely new service models.

For more than a decade, my colleagues and I have helped companies in a variety of industries uncover innovation opportunities by helping them map specific customer jobs and uncover and prioritize the outcomes customers use to measure the successful execution of these jobs. We have come to realize that there are certain patterns to customer jobs. Recognizing these patterns makes the search for core service innovation opportunities more systematic and predictable, as this chapter will show.

Define the Core Job

The starting point in identifying core service innovation opportunities is to define—from the customers' perspective—the core job they are trying to get done by hiring a company's service. What core job does the company's service or services help customers to get done? The core job is the overriding reason the service exists, a specific job the customers are trying to accomplish by hiring the service.[1] Some services clearly target one job; others are hired to help with several jobs. However, even when a customer hires a service to get many jobs done, there is almost always a core job that is the foundation for the accomplishment of the other jobs. So, for example, although investors want to achieve a variety of financial goals, a core job for which a financial adviser is hired that encompasses them all is *develop a financial plan*. In the same way, students have many specific things they want to learn from a class, but the core job, *learn a subject*, encompasses them all.

Recently, when Toronto Dominion (TD) Bank wanted to bring innovation to current services such as checking accounts, savings accounts, and debit and credit cards, it decided to try something different from its old approach, which had been to ask customers for the pros and cons of different banks' accounts. This time, rather than asking questions about banking solutions, TD Bank decided to focus on the customer job.

After internal discussion, the TD innovation team decided that checking accounts, savings accounts, debit and credit cards, and a whole host of other banking services all worked together to help the customer accomplish the core job *manage day-to-day cash flow*. By defining the customer job broadly, the innovation team was able to avoid a myopic focus on current solutions. It discovered opportunities for core service innovation that reached far beyond the traditional scope of TD Bank and its competitors. For example, among the many opportunities the innovation team discovered were those related to making good purchase decisions, paying off short-term debt, and keeping spending on track—opportunities that clearly extended beyond the benefits offered by traditional banking services such as checking and savings accounts. A focus on the day-to-day cash flow job also enabled TD Bank to see that its competitors included not only other banks (or even other financial institutions) but also emerging Internet services such as MyProgress.com and even customer solutions such as placing loose change in jars and keeping a personal record of expenses.

Table 3-1 provides several examples of core job studies that my colleagues and I have investigated in several distinct service industries. Recall from Chapter 1 that job statements (formal expressions of customer jobs) always include a verb followed by a specific object of action, and they may contain a contextual clarifier. A job statement for a core job must abide by the rules of a good job statement and be stated from the customer perspective. Too often, companies define the customer job as what the company offers, but these are not the same. A company offers training, but the customer wants to learn about a topic. A company offers advising, but the customer wants to develop a retirement plan. Training may not be the best way for the customer to learn about a topic, and advising may not be the best way for the customer to develop a retirement plan: a focus on the job rather than its current offerings lets a company develop truly innovative solutions.

Map the Core Job

The next step in identifying core service innovation opportunities is to map—from the customer's perspective—the steps involved in getting a particular core job done.[2] Mapping a job

Table 3-1 Examples of Core Service Innovation Studies

Industry	Customer	Core Job	Outcome Examples
Education	Student	Complete an assignment	• Minimize the time it takes to figure out what information is required to complete an assignment, e.g., what facts and/or statistics • Minimize the likelihood that an assignment is turned in with errors
Financial services	Consumer	Manage day-to-day cash flow	• Minimize the likelihood of forgetting to make a payment • Minimize the time it takes to verify that a payment has been credited
Health care	Surgical nurse	Support surgical case needs for supplies	• Minimize the frequency with which the operating room must be left during a procedure to retrieve additional supplies • Minimize the time it takes to document the supplies used during a procedure

Industry	Customer	Core Job	Outcome Examples
Insurance	Consumer	Manage financial security	• Minimize the likelihood that retirement income fails to keep up with cost-of-living increases • Minimize the loss of income in the event of a disabling illness or accident
Personal services	Consumer	Prepare income tax returns	• Minimize the likelihood that a legitimate credit is excluded from the tax return filing • Minimize the time it takes to verify the accuracy of calculations
Professional services	Research scientist	Retrieve scientific information	• Minimize the time it takes to determine if an answer to a question is accurate • Minimize the number of information sources that must be searched to find an answer to a question
Retail	Marketing executive	Execute an online marketing program	• Minimize the time it takes to determine the optimal size of a purchase incentive • Minimize the cost of validating if a message achieves its objectives

from beginning to end gives a company a complete view of all the points at which a customer might desire value from a product or service. Each of those points offers potential service innovation opportunities.

Regardless of the job or the context in which it's performed, the steps required to get a core job done are virtually the same. This is why we describe our job map as universal: the steps are universally applicable (see Figure 3-1). Specifically, one step in nearly all customer jobs is defining what the job requires; another is locating inputs required to get the job done; others include preparation or setup, confirmation of readiness or priorities, execution, monitoring results and the environment, modification, and one or more concluding steps. In addition, because problems can occur at many points in the process, nearly all jobs require a problem resolution step as well.

The universal job map lessens the likelihood that the company will bound the job incorrectly or overlook a job step. Those steps are important because at each step in the job, customers are looking for certain outcomes—they are assessing how well they're able to get the job done by these outcomes. Any outcome the customer is dissatisfied with represents an opportunity for core service innovation for the company. It's a place where the company can help the customer get the job done better.

This systematic approach was the foundation of Kroll Ontrack's success with its electronic discovery solution, highlighted in the Introduction. Kroll Ontrack mapped the customer job of discovering electronic documents and uncovered outcomes for each step in the job map. The steps included planning for information capture, capturing information, organizing information, marking information, searching information, analyzing the information, and modifying the information.

Figure 3-1 Universal Job Map

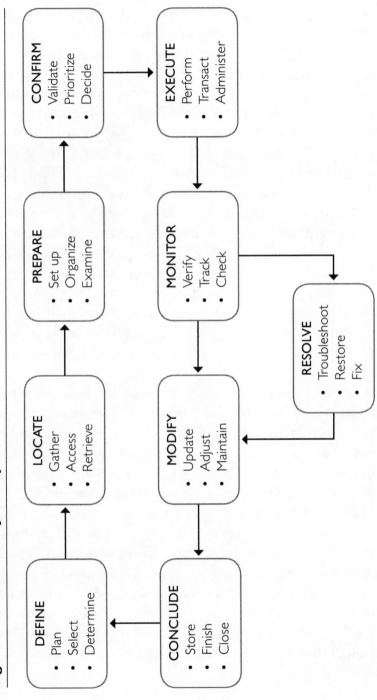

More than 40 outcomes were uncovered from customer interviews. By targeting the outcomes that customers were dissatisfied with, Kroll Ontrack was able to create one of the most sophisticated online review tools in the industry. In addition, specific high-opportunity outcomes led to new services for getting the core job done. The highest opportunity outcome in the Kroll Ontrack study came from the step of capturing information: "Minimize the number of relevant documents that are excluded from capture." In 2007, Kroll Ontrack launched ESI Consulting, which offers clients expert guidance for the task of capturing all relevant documents, from assessing a company's data storage methods to putting together an electronic discovery response plan to helping the client to develop policies and guidelines for managing the entire process.

Job mapping, unlike traditional process mapping, is not about documenting what customers are doing; it is about documenting what they are trying to get done—or better yet, what they must accomplish in order to have success in getting the overall job done. In order to be considered valid, a job step must pass two tests. First, the step must be relevant to anyone doing the job; it is not a valid step if it is relevant only to some of the people doing the job. Again, this is because a valid job step should not be based on how a customer does something but on what they must accomplish. Second, the step must specify what the customer is ultimately trying to accomplish. For example, one person creates a budget and another person checks account balances on a daily basis, but neither of these tasks is a job step because they are not actions taken by all customers doing the job of managing day-to-day cash flow and they do not reflect the more fundamental goal. In the context of managing cash flow, the fundamental goal behind creating a budget is to plan spending, while the fundamental goal behind checking account balances is to confirm the availability of money. These are the job steps, and they align with steps in the universal job map.

The most valuable insight comes from job maps developed from customer interviews. A summary of questions used to create the job map is presented in Table 3-2.

To properly map a customer job, one must ask the right questions—questions regarding what the customer is trying to accomplish at the various points in the process of doing the job and what must happen at those points for the job to be successfully executed. Be careful when tempted to ask about *how* the customer executes the job. This leads to solutions and maps of activities—but not the job the customer is trying to get done.

The following examination of the universal job steps provides general guidance for mapping the steps for a specific job and for searching for opportunities for value creation. However, it is just a guide. When mapping a specific customer job, the steps may use verbs that are different from the ones in Figure 3-1, and you may find that there are multiple steps for a given universal step or even that the steps flow in a different order. By referring to Figure 3-1 and the questions in Table 3-2, however, you can be sure not to miss any key steps when mapping a customer job. Once the job is mapped, you will be ready to discover opportunities for core service innovation.

Define

What must be defined up front to ensure success in getting the overall job done?

The "define" step comprises defining personal and job requirements, planning how to approach the job, determining what resources and inputs are available to complete the job, and selecting what resources to use. Investors might label this step "define financial goals" as they must define investment priorities and risk tolerances; research scientists might label

Table 3-2   Questions Used to Map a Core Job

To find ways to innovate, deconstruct the job a customer is trying to get done. By working through the questions here, you can map a customer job in just a handful of interviews with customers and internal experts.

Start by understanding the execution step, to establish context and a frame of reference. Next, examine each step before execution and then after, to uncover the role each plays in getting the job done.

To ensure that you are mapping job steps (what the customer is trying to accomplish) rather than process solutions (what is currently being done), ask yourself the validating questions at each step.

Validating Questions

As defined, does the step specify what the customer is trying to accomplish (or what must be accomplished), or is it only being done to accomplish a more fundamental goal?

Valid step. Validate employment history.

Invalid step. Call an applicant's past employer.

Does the step apply universally for any customer executing the job, or does it depend on how a particular customer does the job?

Valid step. Monitor investment performance.

Invalid step. Enter investment numbers into a spreadsheet.

Defining the Execution Step

What are the most central tasks that must be accomplished in getting the job done?

• Validate the steps.

Defining Preexecution Steps

What must happen before the core execution step to ensure the job is successfully carried out?

- What must be defined or planned before the execution step?
- What must be located or gathered?
- What must be prepared or set up?
- What must be confirmed before the execution step?
- **Validate the steps.**

Defining Postexecution Steps

What must happen after the core execution step to ensure the job is successfully carried out?

- What must be monitored or verified after the execution step to ensure the job is successfully performed?
- What must be modified or adjusted after the execution step?
- What must be done to properly conclude the job or prepare for the next job cycle?
- **Validate the steps.**

Source: Lance A. Bettencourt and Anthony W. Ulwick, "The Customer-Centered Innovation Map," *Harvard Business Review* 86, no. 5 (May 2008): 109-114.

this step "formulate the research question" as they must identify information needs to have success when searching for scientific information; students might label this step "determine what skills are required" as knowing the skills they need is a prerequisite for success with further study.

At this step, a company can deliver value by helping customers understand their objectives, simplifying the resource planning process, and reducing the amount of planning that is required. Consider how Weight Watchers helps people seeking assistance with the job of losing weight to complete the step of planning meals. To begin, Weight Watchers provides a core weight loss plan that lists all the food choices that are available to the dieter without counting calories, carbohydrates, or anything else. In addition, the program provides the dieter with meal ideas and recipes that fit into its core diet plan. For dieters desiring more flexibility, Weight Watchers provides instant access to point values for over 27,000 foods and provides online tools for assessing the impact of the dieter's favorite recipes.

Locate

What inputs must be located to ensure success in getting the overall job done?

Inputs are both tangible (for example, the surgical tools a nurse must locate for an operation) and intangible (for example, information sources that a research scientist must identify). The "locate" step includes both locating needed inputs and also ensuring that no needed inputs are overlooked and no extraneous inputs are included. The surgical nurse must gather a wide range of surgical tools according to both case characteristics and surgeon preferences; the investor must locate information on potential investment options; the taxpayer must retrieve the various documents and forms required for filing income taxes.

When tangible inputs are involved, a company can add value by finding ways to streamline this step. It might find ways to make the required inputs easier to gather, ensure the inputs are available when and where needed, or make some inputs unnecessary. When intangible inputs such as information are involved, opportunities abound. A company might help customers retrieve stored inputs, facilitate the collection of new inputs, and ensure the thorough and accurate gathering of inputs. Consider how U-Haul helps customers gather the supplies they need in order to complete the job of moving their physical goods. U-Haul provides customers with moving kits that reduce the time it takes to gather the number and types of boxes and supplies that are required for a move, and it also makes all the various supplies a customer might need to move available at a single location. In addition, U-Haul's partnership with eMove makes it possible for customers to quickly locate other types of moving help, such as packers, babysitters, cleaners, and painters.

Prepare

What must be prepared to ensure success in getting the overall job done?

Most customer jobs involve an element of preparing and organizing materials or inputs to the job. The taxpayer filing income taxes must prepare various forms based on an evaluation of available credits and deductions; the research scientist must prepare specific queries to ensure the right types of answers are received during a search; the materials manager must examine replenishment needs before deciding on specific order quantities. Moreover, many customer jobs also entail preparation of the working surface and physical environment in which the job is to be completed. The surgical nurse must prepare the patient and operating room; the teacher must prepare course materials; the software tester must prepare the test environment before running test cases.

With physical inputs, companies should consider services that make setup less cumbersome, that facilitate the organization of physical materials based on how they will be used, or that ensure proper preparation of the inputs required for success. When information is one of the inputs, companies can create value by helping customers organize, integrate, and examine those inputs in a meaningful manner. For example, to help investors compare investment options, RBC Direct Investing provides an online investment comparison tool that allows the investor to create side-by-side comparisons of the various investment options. The comparison describes the basic characteristics of each option, highlights their primary advantages and disadvantages, and indicates which type of risk profile is most aligned with each investment alternative.

Confirm

What must be confirmed to proceed with core job execution and to ensure overall success?

The customer must confirm readiness to begin the actual execution of the job once preparation is complete. This is the point at which the customer ensures that materials and the working environment have been properly prepared, validates the quality and functionality of material and informational inputs, and confirms priorities when it is necessary to decide among execution options. Confirmation is a priority whenever job execution depends on good preparation. So, for example, it is important to a taxpayer to confirm the legitimacy of deductions and credits prior to filing an income tax return, and it is important to the HR function of an organization to confirm a potential employee's background prior to hiring him or her.

A company seeking to offer value at this step should help customers gain access to the types of information and feedback they need to confirm readiness to do the job. It might, for example, help customers choose from among possible options when multiple pathways to job execution are possible (as when they must choose among software designs, shows to watch, purchase options, and so on). A company might also create a solution that builds confirmation into the locating and preparing steps, which would allow the customer to proceed through the first few steps of the job more quickly and easily. Kroll's background screening services, for example, help organizations hire qualified employees by confirming the identities of potential and existing hires, validating professional claims, and identifying any omitted issues that could affect job performance. Kroll ensures the accuracy and completeness of screening services by utilizing a team of specialists from law enforcement, criminal justice, and government service who search primary sources such as public records and speak directly with a job candidate's personal and professional references.

Execute

What must a customer do to execute the core purpose of the job successfully?

The execution step goes by many different names depending on the job. It may be the filing of a tax return, the searching of an information source, the completing of a surgical procedure, or the learning of a skill. Because execution is at the heart of the job, it is central to customers' evaluation of overall success in getting the job done. Opportunities for added value abound at this step, especially in managing two central aspects of every execution process: avoiding problems and optimizing results. An HR manager wants to avoid hiring an employee who will quit due to unrealistic expectations and to optimize the fit between the employee's skills and the job requirements. The person searching for information wants not only to ensure that all relevant information is captured but also to avoid relying on information that is incorrect. A materials manager wants to avoid forgetting to place an order for a surgical case and to optimize the level of inventory for surgical case needs.

Companies can offer value to customers at this step by providing services that offer superior performance regardless of the contextual elements (the when, where, and who) of job execution. There is also considerable opportunity to apply technological know-how to provide real-time feedback to the customer and automatic execution corrections to avoid problems, delays, and bottlenecks in execution and to ensure that optimal results are achieved. H&R Block's TaxCut Signature option for online tax filing provides both technology-enabled support and access to experts to ensure that a tax filer claims all eligible credits and deductions and avoids any filing errors. For those who want to prepare tax returns on their own, the Signature solution includes an online service that automatically checks for errors and provides advice on getting tax benefits based on the taxpayer's life situation. In addition, the Signature option offers the taxpayer the option of tax advice and review of the prepared return by an H&R Block tax professional to ensure that tax returns are filed correctly.

Monitor

What must be monitored to ensure that the job gets done successfully?

For some jobs, the costs of poor execution are significant; for these, monitoring is quite active. With other jobs, monitoring is passive. In either case, monitoring consists of keeping an eye on the results or output from the execution step (including both short-term verification of results and long-term monitoring of performance, when relevant) to see if any adjustments are required to get execution back on track. Often, elements of the job environment also require monitoring to determine when execution adjustments are required. The research scientist searching for specific types of insights must assess the degree to which relevant and complete answers are being returned by search queries and verify when enough information has been gathered; the taxpayer reviews the completed tax return to verify that all eligible credits and deductions have been taken; the consumer tracks expenditures against desired amounts to determine if spending needs to be adjusted to better reflect personal priorities and available funds.

Monitoring activities can be quite time-consuming and demanding. Therefore, services that call attention to any problems in execution or changes in the environment that might require adjustments in job execution are sure to be highly valued. Even more valuable are services that link monitoring with improved job execution or that provide diagnostic feedback. Aetna's MedQuery program delivers just such value to physicians at the monitoring step of treating a patient condition. MedQuery identifies potential omissions in care (missing treatment recommendations) and areas of likely difficulty (such as drug or disease interactions) based on an analysis of Aetna's data (for example, claims and/or patient demographics) and a comparison with the medical community's accepted care guidelines. When an omission or area of difficulty is uncovered, the treating physician is alerted to the opportunity for improved care.

Modify

What modifications are necessary to ensure success in getting the overall job done?

Updates, adjustments, and maintenance are common, especially when there are changes in the inputs or environment in which a job is being executed, when resources or inputs must be maintained and replenished over time, or in response to less-than-optimal output from job execution. The research scientist modifies the elements of a search query to return more relevant answers to a research question; the consumer adjusts planned spending to save more money or to correct problematic spending patterns; the software architect updates application designs when there has been a change in hardware, business processes, or interface technologies.

When modifications or updates are required, customers must decide when, how, what, and where changes should be made. As with monitoring, searching for the right adjustment can be both time-consuming and costly. Therefore, the best services a company can offer at this point are ones that reduce the time it takes to determine when and how to make updates and that reduce the number of adjustment iterations it takes to produce the desired results. In addition, services that target the planning and preparation steps can be designed to cut down on the frequency or number of modifications needed, or even to eliminate them altogether. A very good example of value being delivered at this step is the Martin's Point Health Coach Service, a service available to anyone enrolled in health plans managed by Martin's Point. Customers who are dealing with a specific health concern can call a toll-free number and speak with a specially trained health professional who can provide the guidance needed to make more informed health decisions, including adjustments to diet, exercise, and lifestyle.

Conclude

What must the customer do to successfully conclude the job?

With some simple jobs, tasks related to executing and concluding the job are closely intertwined. With more complex jobs, there are often one or more distinct steps required to finish the job successfully. The investor must store investment information for later use; the student learning a new skill must put the skill into use; the prospective homeowner must close on the home; the software architect must hand off design plans to others in the development sequence. The conclusion of a job is a good point at which to offer customers value for two reasons. First, many jobs are cyclical in nature, so the conclusion of one job cycle is often the beginning of another cycle—or at least, the conclusion of one cycle has an impact on the beginning of the next cycle. Second, people often dislike dealing with concluding steps because the core job has already been completed and they would like to move on.

When a job is cyclical, one way to offer value is by making sure that concluding activities are closely connected to the starting point of a new job cycle. Storing documents, for example, should facilitate retrieving documents. And, as with any step, anything that can be done to facilitate the concluding step will add value. PayPal, for example, adds considerable value to the concluding step of selling items on the Internet by facilitating the efficient receipt of payments from the buyer. Through proprietary risk models, seller protections, and direct links to buyer and seller financial accounts, PayPal reduces the time it takes the seller to receive payment, increases the number of payment options the seller can accept, reduces the likelihood of selling to a fraudulent buyer, and reduces the possibility of financial loss due to unauthorized payments or claims of items not being received.

Resolve

What problems related to getting the overall job done must be resolved on occasion?

Even in the simplest of jobs, things occasionally go wrong that halt the execution of the job—orders are late, income taxes are audited, travel plans get canceled, and dieters gain unexpected weight. When this happens, the customer must disengage from the core job process and undertake the ancillary job of resolving the problem at hand. What customers want at this point is a speedy resolution, and speed of resolution is often a function of taking the right approach to dealing with the problem. How should a taxpayer who has been notified of an audit prepare for the audit? If a nurse receives a cut during a surgical operation, what steps should he or she take to prevent becoming infected with a bloodborne disease? If an item is received damaged, how should a return to the vendor be handled?

When problems occur, companies can add value by guiding customers through the entire job of resolving the problem, including providing support and diagnostics to assess the problem and resources to resolve the problem, ensuring that the resolution protects the customer and other resources that might be affected, and providing the customer with verification that the problem has been resolved. Services that target and eliminate problems that might occur at each job step offer obvious value. Priority Traveller, a service that caters to travelers, includes among its offerings help in resolving problems that can occur while taking a trip. If a member loses luggage, Priority Traveller tracks the luggage down and keeps the member informed every step along the way. A travel insurance policy also covers expenses for a variety of problems that might be encountered on a trip, including hospitalization, accidental loss of business equipment, loss of deposit for unused travel, and accommodations when one misses a departure.

Uncover Outcomes

Once a customer job has been mapped, a company is ready to begin capturing outcomes. Customers use their desired outcomes to measure their success in getting a job done. The job map is an excellent tool for helping to uncover these outcomes because at each step on the job map, customers will have a number of desired outcomes.

One very important foundation for capturing customer outcomes is recognizing that customers consider only three types of outcomes when they evaluate a job: those related to input, process, and output. This makes intuitive sense given that jobs are processes and job steps are subprocesses. The primary focus of input outcomes is speed—reduced time to complete something related to getting the job done (for example, *minimize the time it takes to determine if a specific expense is deductible*). On occasion, however, there are also other focuses for input outcomes including reduced mental effort or reduced number of supplies required, and so on. The primary focus of process outcomes is reduced variability—elimination of problems, bottlenecks, and so on that cause job execution to go off track (for example, *minimize the likelihood that a legitimate deduction is overlooked*). Finally, the primary focus of output outcomes is optimized results (for example, *minimize the likelihood that a claimed deduction triggers an IRS audit*).

With the job as the anchor and recognition that input, process, and output are the three primary types of outcomes, it is easy to ask customers questions that will elicit the outcomes that they use to measure success. For each step in a job map, ask these questions:

- What makes [this step] time-consuming or slow? What makes it cumbersome or inconvenient?
- What makes [this step] problematic or challenging? What causes it to be inconsistent or to go off track?
- What makes [this step] ineffective or the output of poor quality? What would the ideal result look like?

You will recall that customers hire solutions to help them get a job done and that outcomes are the hiring criteria by which competing solutions are evaluated. Because customers use outcomes when choosing from among solutions, it is possible to uncover outcomes by exploring with customers the reasons behind the solution choices they make when getting a job done. As such, a very productive question to ask is "What makes one solution better or worse than another when getting [this step] done?" As with jobs, the person asking the questions must be willing to probe until a metric on the job is uncovered that can be phrased in a way that complies with the rules for a good outcome statement. Although the line of questioning is straightforward, uncovering high-quality outcome statements takes some work by a trained interviewer.

To capture outcomes, we rely on a combination of one-on-one interviews, small group interviews, and observational interviews. As with jobs, customers can articulate the outcomes they desire even when there are no product or service solutions available to get the job done. If customers are somehow managing to do the job, even if by relying on makeshift, do-it-yourself solutions, then they know where there are issues of delays, problems, and poor-quality results. All you have to do is ask the right questions with the right frame of reference—the job.

From a dozen interviews with a diverse group of customers, a trained interviewer can uncover 80 to 120 or more distinct outcomes that customers use to measure success in getting a job done. With this list of outcomes, a company knows exactly how customers judge value when getting the job done. Next, the company must identify the outcomes that are most important to customers but which customers are currently unsatisfied with. It is those important, unsatisfactory outcomes that offer the best opportunities for core service innovation.

When we worked with TD Bank to uncover customer outcomes for the job of managing day-to-day cash flow, we talked to approximately 50 consumers using a combination of personal and group interviews to uncover a total of 82 outcomes spread out over more than 10 core job steps. Examination of high-opportunity outcomes related to setting aside money for savings, including increasing the likelihood that a planned amount is set aside for savings each pay period, led to the Simply Save program. The Simply Save program helps a customer set money aside by putting a specified amount of money into a savings account every time the customer uses a TD Bank debit card for a purchase or withdrawal. The customer decides the amount to set aside with each transaction, and the money goes into the savings account of the customer's choice. An online calculator helps customers to estimate what they will save by participating in the program.

Define a Core Job across Complementary Solutions

When a company is taking stock of its current services and contemplating core service innovation, the starting point is to ask, "What job does our service or our services help a customer to get done?" The responses to this question will come at several levels of abstraction. For example, one person might answer that customers hire the company's services to pay bills, while another might say that customers hire the company's services to manage day-to-day cash flow—and both may be right. What is often the case is that the job as stated at the lower level of abstraction is actually a job step in accomplishing the higher-order job. Paying bills, for example, is actually one step in the job of managing day-to-day cash flow. To get the higher-order job done, customers generally rely on several distinct but complementary solutions. This means that a company whose services customers currently employ to help with one step in the higher-order job can find many opportunities by focusing on other steps in the process of accomplishing the higher-order job. This is especially true when the customer hands over job execution to the service provider when the service is hired, as in the case of auto repair, interior design, and so on.

Given the benefit of identifying a higher-level job, it's clear a company should take initial core job definitions and ask, "Is this job [Are these jobs] part of a higher-level job that would offer more service innovation insight?" and "Is there a job for which our services are complementary to others?" For example, Kroll Ontrack offers services for recovering lost data. However, rather than consider *recover lost data* the customer job, it may make more sense for Kroll Ontrack to recognize this as the problem resolution step of the higher-order job *protect against the loss of data,* which includes steps for planning, implementation, and monitoring that can lead to entirely new services. Similarly, Elsevier offers services for searching for scientific information. However, rather than define the job as *search for information,* it may be better to see this as the "locate" step of the higher-order job *conduct scholarly research,* which includes steps for developing research questions, selecting a publication outlet, and writing an article, any of which Elsevier could target for service innovation. As a final example, Travelocity offers services that help customers make travel reservations. However, rather than define the job as *make travel reservations,* it may be better to recognize this as the preparation step of the higher-order job *take a trip,* which includes steps for travel planning, taking the trip, and returning home, all of which are open for service innovation.

Define a Core Job across Substitutes

A company searching for meaningful core service innovation should also fight the temptation to define the core job around obtaining a particular service—or even service at all. You will recognize that you have fallen into this trap if your job statement relies on verbs that are synonymous with *obtain* such as *get, take, receive,* and *have,* or if your job definition refers to a service or service provider. Examples of these deficient core job statements include *get a haircut, have money invested, stay at a hotel, have a home built, receive health care services, get advice from a lawyer,* and *attend a show.* Chapter 4, which focuses specifically on innovation in service delivery, introduces a universal job map for obtaining service—a job map that presumes service as a solution. The job statements listed above would be fine within those parameters. Right now, however, we want to look more broadly.

One way to fight the temptation to define the core job around service is to consider a job definition that encompasses complementary solutions, as described above. Another is to define the job across substitutes—that is, to define the job in a way that makes it possible for products as well as different types of services to offer useful solutions. In many markets, services are the primary way to get a job done, but in others, services are only a small fraction of the solutions that customers hire to get the job done. It is in these markets especially that a company will want to define the customer's core job in a way that encompasses substitute solutions to getting the job done. For example, the job of saving money applies equally well to customers who hire a bank and customers who hire mattresses and jars. The job of learning about a topic applies equally well to customers who hire eLearning, in-person training, and a book off the shelf. And the job of diagnosing a health condition applies as much to customers who hire WebMD as to those who hire an in-the-flesh doctor.

Once a job is defined across substitutes, its steps must be mapped in a way that applies across substitutes, and outcomes must be captured to reflect how customers evaluate success independent of which solutions they hire. This will mean that the outcome statements are more abstract, but this course of action will prove invaluable to a company that wants to discover core service innovation opportunities that appeal not only to service customers but also to product customers and noncustomers who are also trying to get the job done.

Relate Outcomes to Emotional Jobs

Chapter 2 revealed how a company can uncover customers' emotional jobs, and this chapter has shown how to uncover the outcomes that customers use to measure success when getting a particular job done. But how are outcomes and emotional jobs related?

Emotional jobs do not have outcomes. Instead, customers' success in getting emotional jobs done is influenced by their success in getting the core job done. For example, my ability to feel confident (an emotional job) when doing the job of losing weight is contingent upon how satisfied I am with the outcomes of the core job—for example, how well current solutions help me to minimize the time it takes to determine if a particular food can be eaten as part of a diet and to minimize the likelihood of having cravings for unhealthy foods. In other words, when a solution better satisfies the outcomes on getting a core job done, it also helps the customer satisfy his or her emotional jobs.

In pursuing core service innovation opportunities, a company will generally want to know which emotional jobs are tied to high-opportunity outcomes for the core job. A simple way to determine which emotional jobs are most strongly related to specific outcomes is to correlate the satisfaction ratings of outcomes and emotional jobs from the survey.[3] Once a company knows which emotional jobs are most highly correlated with the high-opportunity outcomes, then any service innovations that it develops to address the core job can also be designed to take those emotional jobs into account. For example, when TD Bank looked at which emotional jobs were most strongly correlated with the top outcome opportunities for managing day-to-day cash flow, it discovered that core service innovations targeting these outcomes should also be positioned to emphasize the emotional jobs *feel worry free* and *feel confident*. If a company's brand image is tied to specific emotional jobs, then the reverse process—determining which outcomes are most strongly related to those emotional jobs—can also help a company to choose among outcome opportunities for core service innovation.

SUMMARY

Core service innovation relies on the discovery of opportunities to help customers get a particular job done better. To do this, a company must first define the core job for which customers are hiring current services. To gain the most innovation insight, the customer job should be defined in a way that encompasses complementary solutions and substitutes. This will help the company innovate not only by improving current services but also by creating new, complementary services.

The company's innovations will focus on opportunities to help the customer to get the core job done better. These opportunities may exist at any of the steps that customers must accomplish to get the overall job done. The universal job map helps companies discover these opportunities. Because job mapping does not document what customers are doing, but rather what they must accomplish in order to complete a job successfully, it can lead to the discovery of many core service innovation opportunities. However, to provide even richer insight, a company should also uncover and prioritize the outcomes that customers use to measure success at each step in the customer job. Outcomes that customers feel are important but with which they are unsatisfied represent prime opportunities for core service innovation.

CHAPTER 4

DISCOVER OPPORTUNITIES FOR SERVICE DELIVERY INNOVATION

Service delivery innovation focuses on improving how customers obtain the benefits of a service. This is narrowly focused innovation: it's not a search for a brand new solution but rather a search for ways to improve an existing service. Once customers decide to hire a service to get a job done, they begin the process of "consuming" the benefits of the service offering. Once I decide upon a particular auto insurance to protect against financial loss in the event of an accident (the core job), there are a number of things that must happen for me to obtain the benefits of auto insurance. I must make the initial contact, define my coverage, and, if I have the misfortune of being in an accident, I must file a claim and receive the promised benefits. In this chapter, rather than focusing on the core customer job, we will focus on the consumption chain job of obtaining service.

This chapter introduces a universal job map for the consumption chain job of obtaining service. This job map is as relevant to discovering opportunities to improve service delivery at a fast-food restaurant as it is to discovering opportunities to improve service delivery in commercial banking. It provides a systematic approach for any company wanting to discover innovation opportunities in service delivery. With the universal job map in hand, a company knows what must happen for a customer to receive service benefits and has a guide to understand how customers define success at every step along the way.

The Universal Job Map for Obtaining Service

Unlike a core job, the consumption chain job of obtaining service should be defined with a particular service or group of complementary services in mind. The focus is the customer's consumption of the service, whether the service being consumed is a primary service (for example, providing hotel accommodations) or a subservice (for example, providing room service to people staying at the hotel).

Just as a core job should be defined in a solution-independent manner, the consumption chain job of obtaining service should generally be defined in a manner that is independent of the form of service delivery (for example, in person versus via the Internet or self-service versus full service). This is because as soon as you define how the service is delivered (a solution to how service is obtained), you are restricting the field of innovation discovery to that form of delivery. Restricting the form of the service delivery also limits the company's ability to compare the advantages and disadvantages of distinct forms of service delivery.[1]

A job statement for obtaining service, like a core job statement, should always begin with a verb followed by a specific object of action. The statement should also be worded from the customer's perspective. As discussed in Chapter 3, a job statement for obtaining service will often begin with verbs such as *obtain, get, take, receive,* and *have* (though not exclusively), and it will either imply or directly refer to the service or service benefits that are being obtained.

Below are some job statements that involve the obtaining of services:

- Take a class (education)
- Get a home built (construction)
- Obtain health care services (health care)
- Receive Internet access (utilities)
- Rent a car (retail)
- Obtain a commercial loan (finance)
- Stay at a hotel (hospitality)
- Take a flight (transportation)
- Attend an event (entertainment)
- Get clothes laundered (personal services)

Once the job is defined, the next task is to map—from the customer's perspective—the steps involved in getting the job of obtaining service done. This is how a company gains a complete view of all the points at which a customer might derive value from improved service delivery processes. With that knowledge in hand, a company can then offer service delivery innovations that create customer value and allow the company to differentiate itself competitively at any given step in the job or for the job as a whole.

A universal job map for obtaining service is presented in Figure 4-1. This universal job map builds on the core job map presented in Chapter 3, but it is tailored to the job of obtaining service. This enables greater specificity in the steps, although some steps are likely to be relevant to certain services and not others. We'll consider these variations as the individual steps are discussed.

As shown in Figure 4-1, the job begins with the step of defining service needs, which may take place before the service pro-

Figure 4-1 Universal Job Map for Obtaining Service

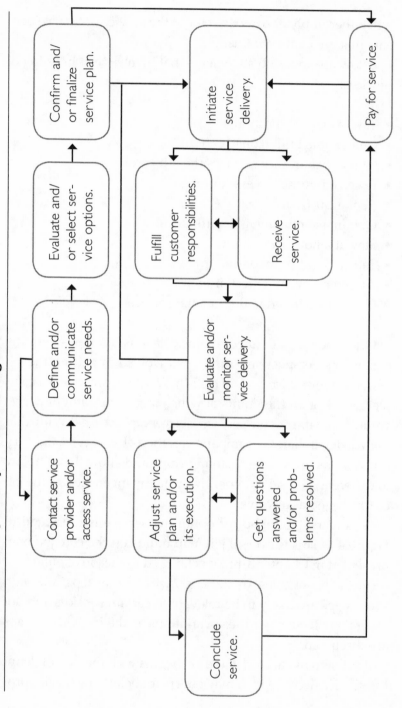

vider is even contacted. The job of obtaining service ends with one or more activities to conclude the service. In between are such activities as contacting and/or accessing the service provider, evaluating and/or selecting service options, finalizing a service plan and/or initiating service delivery, fulfilling customer responsibilities, receiving service benefits, evaluating and/or monitoring service delivery, adjusting the service plan and/or its execution, occasionally getting questions answered or problems resolved, and paying for the service.[2]

Readers familiar with service blueprinting may see a resemblance between the obtaining service job map illustrated in Figure 4-1 and the customer action component of a service blueprinting process map. To be sure, they do share some commonalities. In particular, both approaches provide a means of visualizing a service as a process. However, the focus of a job map is different. A service blueprint creates a visual representation of how a service is delivered.[3] The goal is to capture significant service encounters and interactions for distinct customer segments. It is most useful for service design and development. In contrast, a job map creates a visual representation of what a customer must accomplish to obtain the service and its benefits. A job map does not map service encounters; it maps the purposes behind the encounters and the steps a customer must take to have success obtaining service. A job map is most useful for service delivery innovation, though it is also valuable during service design.

Guided by the universal job map for obtaining service, a company can create a job map for a specific service from just a handful of personal interviews. Not many interviews are required because the company already knows what steps to look for when mapping the job and because every customer interview can provide rich insight into the entire job due to the focus on what *must* be done. Once the job has been mapped, the company can gain additional insight into service delivery innovation opportunities from capturing the specific outcomes that customers use to judge success at each step in consuming a particular service. It can also begin to think of innovative ways to differentiate its service delivery for every step in the job. A summary of questions used to create the job map is presented in Table 4-1.

Table 4-1   Questions Used to Map the Job of Obtaining Service

To find ways to innovate, deconstruct the job a customer is trying to get done. By working through the questions here, you can map the customer's job of obtaining service in just a handful of interviews with customers and internal experts.

Like a core job, you can start by understanding the "receive service" step, to establish context and a frame of reference. However, for this job, it may be preferable to start at the beginning of the job map and work your way through each of the steps, to define what each means for your service.

To ensure that you are mapping job steps (what the customer is trying to accomplish) rather than process solutions (what is currently being done), ask yourself the validating questions at each step.

Validating Questions

As defined, does the step specify what the customer is trying to accomplish (or what must be accomplished), or is the step being done to accomplish only a more fundamental goal?

Valid step. Apply for a loan.
Invalid step. Fill out loan paperwork.

Does the step apply universally for any customer executing the job, or does it depend on how a particular customer does the job?

Valid step. Place an order.
Invalid step. Call the supplier to place an order.

Defining Preobtaining Service Steps

What must happen before service benefits are received to ensure success obtaining service and/or its benefits?

- What contact or access to the service is required?
- What service needs must be defined or communicated by the customer before service is received?
- What options must be evaluated or selected?
- What must be finalized, understood, or approved?
- **Validate the steps.**

Defining the Obtaining Service Steps

What must happen for the customer to obtain service and/or its benefits?

- What must the customer do to initiate service delivery?
- What responsibilities must the customer fulfill to ensure success?
- What service delivery or other service contacts must the customer receive?
- **Validate the steps.**

Defining Postobtaining Service Steps

What must happen after service benefits are received to ensure success obtaining service and/or its benefits?

- What must be monitored or evaluated by the customer during or after service is received?
- What adjustments in the service plan or delivery must the customer initiate or execute?
- What questions or problems related to service delivery must the customer have addressed?
- What must the customer do to conclude the service or maintain the service relationship over time?
- What payment actions are required of the customer?
- **Validate the steps.**

We helped Ceridian Corporation, a global business services company, follow this approach to service innovation in their quest to understand the needs of HR executives who used Ceridian's outsourcing services. Ceridian positions itself as "the best care in the industry." To that end, we interviewed 30 HR executives to map the job of outsourcing human resources. The job map included steps such as defining service needs with the service provider, understanding the impact of HR outsourcing, implementing a new service arrangement, supporting the outsourcing service, managing HR transactions, adapting to changes in company requirements, and supporting employee needs. Following prioritization of more than 40 outcomes, Ceridian discovered several opportunities to improve its service delivery.

One key service delivery innovation Ceridian introduced had to do with defining service needs and helping customers understand the service plan. Ceridian developed service standards and detailed process flows for its service delivery model that help customers visualize the service and make it easier for them to discuss their requirements at each step along the way. Ceridian also relies on the standards to help clients understand what service will be like, make informed recommendations to clients about best practices, and ensure that unique client requirements are understood within the service organization. As a result, Ceridian has been able to address several customer outcomes related to outsourcing human resources, including minimizing the likelihood that the vendor misunderstands customer requirements, minimizing the number of outsourcing implementation details that are not communicated to the client, and minimizing the difference between the estimated and actual implementation times. Ceridian now has an internal team devoted to updating and creating new service standards. Ceridian's customer advisory board and improved Net

Promoter scores indicate that the standards have significantly improved initial customer satisfaction.

In addition, Ceridian discovered that customers were concerned about the effort required to move data to and from Ceridian's hosted HR and payroll system and their internal operational systems. Prior to the study, details on data movement were established for each outsourcing engagement, resulting in very labor intensive and error prone processes. After understanding customers' concerns, Ceridian not only found ways to help customers reduce their workload but also to improve the reliability of its own service. In particular, Ceridian introduced a set of tools to automate and schedule the data movement processes. Describing the benefits of this approach to service innovation, Lance Reschke, vice president of human resource outsourcing, said, "It's not about driving the *how*. It's really about the *what*—what is the customer trying to accomplish, and how can Ceridian best respond to the customer's needs? This effort and Ceridian's overall focus on the customer are opening doors for us, to explore more options and ways to solve a problem than we would have discovered with a typical satisfaction survey."[4]

The following discussion of the universal job steps for obtaining service provides general guidance for mapping a specific job and for informing service delivery innovation. When mapping the job for a specific service, the steps may have somewhat different labels from those in Figure 4-1, and you may find that there are multiple steps for a given universal step, that the steps flow in a slightly different order, or that some steps should be combined because they happen concurrently. This is to be expected. The universal job map is simply a general guide. By referring to Figure 4-1 and the questions in Table 4-1, however, you can be sure not to miss any key steps.

Contact Service Provider and/or Access Service

What contact or access to the service is required by the customer to ensure success obtaining service and/or its benefits?

To obtain service, customers must contact the service provider and/or access its services. This includes knowing when and how to initiate contact, making appointments, and getting to the service provider (the company, specific individuals, and specific locations), and it encompasses both physical and virtual access. For many services, contact or access happens every time the service is hired—for example, each time customers want to purchase groceries or attend an event, they must access the service and the parts of the service that make doing those jobs possible. For services in which there is an explicit or implicit long-term service plan (for example, auto insurance or banking), initial contacts with the service provider happen as part of defining the services to be offered, and subsequent contacts are to engage the services offered by the provider.

When contacting a service provider or accessing its services, customers are looking for convenient access, which means few restrictions on when, where, and how they can access or contact the service, fast access at every point at which contact is necessary, and knowledge of how to make contact or access the service for what they are trying to accomplish. In addition, customers want that access to be safe and secure. Virgin Atlantic's Upper Class service meets those needs for first-class passengers. A complimentary chauffeur-driven car takes the passenger to the airport. Once at the airport, the passenger can bypass the terminal with a special drive-through check-in program that lets the passenger proceed straight to a first-class clubhouse. Passengers who want to minimize the amount of time they spend at the airport can arrive as late as 40 minutes before departure and proceed through a special security channel to the boarding gate.

Define and/or Communicate Service Needs

What service needs or inputs must the customer define or communicate to ensure success obtaining service and/or its benefits?

To ensure success in obtaining service, customers must define the needs they want the service to satisfy before they can select a particular service option. For many low-risk, familiar, and self-service situations (for example, shipping a package, taking a flight, replenishing inventory), customers define their service needs prior to contacting the service provider. With more complex services (for example, receiving medical care or building a financial plan), in contrast, customers define their needs through communication with the service provider following initial contact.

Even for simple services, a service provider can add value by helping customers to define their service needs. To be successful, the customer wants to have the right inputs available for making decisions, not overlook any relevant needs, limit the costs of defining needs (including personal costs, such as embarrassment), and define the needs in a manner that can translate into decisions concerning service options. To ensure that its customers get an optimized treatment plan for their lawn, for example, the field staff of Scotts LawnService uncover a lawn's unique challenges through a detailed analysis of soil types, shade and sun exposure, types of weeds, and varying levels of grass density.

On the communication side of things, a service provider can offer value by keeping in mind that customers want to share all information that is required but no more than that, that they don't want to have to give out the same information multiple times, and that they want to make their needs understood in as few interactions with the provider as possible. Allstate, for example, offers an online tool that allows a prospective customer to get a ballpark estimate of the cost of auto insurance coverage with five simple questions and no sharing of personal information. Allstate also offers a free personal quote online.

Evaluate and/or Select Service Options

What options must be evaluated and/or selected by the customer to ensure success obtaining service and/or its benefits?

Customers must evaluate the service options available to them and select from among the choices based on their needs. This step covers not only what services are selected but also when, where, and how services are obtained. In self-service situations, the customer may simply review lists of service options, as in a restaurant or when making travel reservations. In other situations, the service provider may present the customer with various options, based on an understanding of the customer's specific service needs. This is the case with car repair, medical treatment, and obtaining a commercial loan.

This can be a particularly challenging step because it is difficult to try a service and therefore difficult to evaluate a service beforehand. Companies can help by making informed recommendations, facilitating quick and objective comparisons among options, helping the customer to anticipate what the service might be like, and using language the customer can understand. When evaluating service options, customers want to know what options are available, be aware of the cost implications of different options, and understand the when, where, how, and why of different service options. Ultimately, they want to have confidence that they are making the best choice for their situation. To help with this step, Aetna offers an interactive online benefit adviser that asks questions about family situation, current health status, and savings availability and then recommends the plan that most likely fits the needs of the prospective customer. A very personable virtual adviser then explains the benefits and costs of the recommended Aetna plan and why Aetna recommends that particular plan for the customer. If there are questions that the adviser cannot answer, customers may submit contact information for follow-up by an Aetna representative.

Confirm and/or Finalize Service Plan

What plans must be finalized, understood, or approved by the customer to ensure success obtaining service and/or its benefits?

Once service options have been selected, many services require an explicit service agreement before service benefits can be obtained. For example, an auto insurance customer must apply for a policy, a human resource executive must agree to terms of an outsourcing engagement, and a rental car customer must sign a rental agreement. Other services rely on implicit agreements between the service provider and the customer. For example, a patient must agree to a treatment plan before it can be implemented, and customers often have to finalize payment or service details before a purchase can be made. When a service is complex or relies on unique terminology, as with medical care and health insurance, customers may not easily be able to ensure that a service agreement meets their needs and fulfills promises. These situations present the service company with ample opportunity to fail or delight the customers.

Whether the agreement is explicit or implicit, customers want to be sure that they understand it. They want to avoid being oversold; they want to pay the least possible amount for the services received, and they want to avoid being taken advantage of. Customers also want to limit the number of restrictions on services, make sure the final agreement reflects prior promises, and ensure that there is nothing hidden in the agreement. De Mar, a plumbing, heating, and air-conditioning company in Clovis, California, has achieved considerable success by targeting these needs. De Mar keeps its agreement with customers simple and fair: it not only guarantees the price of repairs to the penny before any work begins, it also guarantees all parts and labor for one year.

Initiate Service Delivery

What must the customer do to initiate service delivery to ensure success obtaining service and/or its benefits?

In many transactional services, the activity that initiates service delivery is placing an order or communicating a request for service. This is true when getting a haircut, requesting room service, and filling a prescription, for example. Even when the customer does not have service options—for example, when requesting an ambulance—service begins with this step. Placing an order is to a transactional service what finalizing a service plan is to a relational service (although some services require both steps). A service provider can add value at this stage by simplifying the process of placing an order and by ensuring that the order is accurate and complete. One-click ordering, for example, was an important service delivery innovation for Amazon. After the customer's first order with Amazon, selecting the 1-Click button on any product page allows the customer to skip entry of order information by defaulting to the customer's preferred payment method and shipping address.

There may be a time gap between when an agreement is put in place and when certain benefits of a service are obtained. With auto insurance, for example, the agreement may be in place for months or years before service delivery is initiated through the filing of a claim. With a commercial loan, the agreement may be in place long before a request for funds is made. In these cases, when the time eventually comes for the customer to initiate service delivery, the customer essentially proceeds with the "contact" step again and has similar concerns as when making the initial contact and communicating service needs.

Some services require setup or learning after an agreement is in place but before services are received. When customers contract for Internet access, for example, or outsource HR needs, initiating service delivery involves learning and setup. In such situations, customers want to accomplish the following:

- Know what actions to take
- Reduce the time it takes to be ready for service delivery
- Minimize the costs and other negative impacts of setup
- Limit the number of changes (to equipment, procedures, and so on) that are required to receive service

Consider how eBay adds value at this step. In addition to a prominent "New to Selling?" link that leads to helpful information on selling basics and creating effective listings, eBay guides the new seller through the process of listing an item for sale step-by-step. Finally, for services that entail work on physical objects (for example, pet grooming or auto repair), an important part of initiating service delivery is providing the inputs required for service (for example, a pet or a car).

Fulfill Customer Responsibilities

What responsibilities must the customer fulfill to ensure success obtaining service and/or its benefits?

Service customers often play a part in their own service delivery. They become partners of the service provider when getting ready to receive service, making service happen, and keeping service going. A patient must follow a treatment regimen for it to have its intended effect; a tax-return customer must gather account information, receipts, and other documents if a CPA is to file the customer's taxes; a student must complete assignments. In addition, some customers who are professionals rely on another firm's service to fulfill the needs of their own customers, and they have many of their own responsibilities to fulfill.

When customers have responsibilities to fulfill, they need to know what to do, they must have the skills and resources to fulfill their role, and they must be sufficiently motivated to do so. Customers want to reduce the time and costs associated with their role. Weight Watchers addresses those needs by offering various online and mobile tools to help dieters track food activity, chart progress, make meals that fit the plan, and stay motivated wherever they are.

Companies should be careful, however, to distinguish between what a customer does today to receive service and what must be done. It may well be that some steps that the customer currently does could be taken over by the service provider—a clear benefit for the customer. For example, Progressive's concierge service has broken the mold of what the customer does to get a car repaired after an accident. All the customer needs to do is drop off his or her car at a Progressive service center, and Progressive takes care of the rest, from arranging repairs with a body shop, monitoring repair progress, and even inspecting repair quality.

Receive Service

What service delivery or other service contacts must the customer receive to ensure success obtaining service and/or its benefits?

Whether the service is transactional or relational in nature, the benefits to be received tie back to the customer's service plan or order request. What is received goes by many different names. A commercial loan customer receives funds. A patient receives treatment. A student receives instruction. A utilities customer receives power. An insurance customer receives protection. More generally, a service customer can receive physical changes, ownership changes, location changes, personal-state changes, information or guidance, or protection against such changes. In addition, the customer must often receive communications and other documents as part of obtaining service. When the customer is obtaining service on behalf of someone else, this step might be considered as providing something, as when a benefits manager provides coverage to employees based on an agreement they have put into place with an insurance carrier.

When receiving service delivery, customers want fast and complete resolution of problems or accomplishment of goals—the job for which the service is hired. They want the service provider to fulfill its promises in a way that is most suited to their needs, and they want to avoid any complications, inconveniences, or mistakes along the way. TelaDoc, a telephone-based medical consultation and diagnosis service, addresses these needs by guaranteeing a return call from a physician within 3 hours or the medical consultation is free. Medical consultation is available by telephone 24 hours a day, all year round.

When services are delivered in a physical facility, customers will also judge the success of the service in terms of outcomes related to facility cleanliness, navigation, and interactions with the facility (and possibly other customers). In addition, customers want to have services available when and where they want, and they are looking to limit the personal costs (financial, physical, social, and so on) associated with receiving those services. The fitness franchise Curves addressed the service delivery needs of women who wanted to become physically fit, providing equipment that was designed for women's comfort and that didn't require users to be fitness experts. Further, by providing an all-female exercise environment, Curves removed the stress that many women experienced when working out around men.

Evaluate and/or Monitor Service Delivery

What evaluation or monitoring is required by the customer to ensure success obtaining service and/or its benefits?

There are many different types of evaluation or monitoring that might be required of the customer to ensure success with obtaining service. If the service involves a service plan agreement, the customer must review it and verify the details of the plan, and possibly also verify that the service was delivered as specified. For some services, customers don't actually observe the service being delivered (for example, when an insurance company takes care of a claim or when an automatic payment is made from a checking account), so in those situations, they want to verify that the service delivery has taken place or is progressing. To address this need, Scotts LawnService leaves a notice on the customer's door each time a lawn care visit takes place. The notice details what treatments were applied, what each treatment was, what to expect, and what the customer should do next.

In addition, customers want to know if a service has had its intended effect. Customers who have had their car repaired want to confirm that the repair has truly fixed the car, for example. But the benefits received from many services are intangible and difficult to assess, which means a service provider can add value by helping customers determine if they have received the benefits they sought. Customers also appreciate help determining if there are problems that require remediation, which is the need credit card companies are addressing when they alert customers to unusual charges. Similarly, Terminix, the pest control service, helps its customers to verify service quality by including an annual inspection with its termite extermination services. If the inspection reveals that the termite problem persists, Terminix will re-treat the home at no extra cost to the homeowner.

Adjust Service Plan and/or Its Execution

What adjustments in the service plan or its execution are initiated by the customer to ensure success obtaining service and/or its benefits?

There are various reasons why the customer might need the service plan or the execution of the service to be changed. The customer might require adjustments to the terms of a service plan if problems with the agreement are discovered. Or the customer might simply want to update personal information or add or change service options to accommodate a change in personal situation—for example, a customer might wish to add a car to an auto insurance policy or reallocate funds in an investment portfolio. Sometimes a customer wants to update the service provider about changes in his or her situation that will affect what, when, where, and how services should be received. For example, a company outsourcing its HR function must update the service provider not only about new hires but also about changes in corporate policy that affect how the provider delivers services. Finally, with any service in which the customer has the opportunity to monitor and evaluate results, the customer may want to request changes to the service being delivered, such as when a restaurant patron requests changes in how food has been prepared.

When adjustments are required, the customer will value a service that makes it clear how to make changes and enables changes to be made quickly, with no mistakes, and at low cost. Expedia, for example, has recently removed change and cancellation fees on all hotel, car rental, and cruise reservations and on nearly all flight reservations made on Expedia.com. Sometimes, customers may not realize they could benefit by making a change. This is another opportunity for a service provider to offer value: for example, Travelocity's PriceGuardian service automatically monitors prices and refunds a price difference to the customer if another customer books the same flight and hotel package for less.

Get Questions Answered and/or Problems Resolved

What questions or problems related to service delivery must the customer have addressed to ensure success obtaining service and/or its benefits?

When problems occur, as they inevitably will, customers first and foremost want a fast, fair, and convenient resolution to the problem. This requires that customers understand what actions to take and have multiple contact and problem resolution options available to them. The same principles apply when the customer has a question. The approach that the Gaylord Palms hotel in Orlando, Florida, takes to these needs is notable: it has equipped each guest room with a phone that has a "Consider It Done" button. By pressing "Consider It Done," a guest can question hotel staff on a wide range of topics, request a wide range of services, and "consider it done."

When contacting the service provider, customers want to initiate the contact at their convenience. They do not want to have to make multiple contacts, and they do not want to be intimidated or made to feel embarrassed when communicating with the service provider. They want to know what progress is being made to resolve their problem or answer their question, and they want the resolution to be prompt. This is true whether the problem is caused by the service provider or not. Consider how Mastercard handles customer problems. In addition to its zero-liability policy, Mastercard provides downloadable contact numbers so customers who lose a card while traveling know exactly how to contact Mastercard to report the loss. This service is provided 24/7, 365 days a year in the language of the customer's choice. Once contacted, Mastercard Global Service can provide emergency cash advances, direction to ATMs in the surrounding area, and an emergency replacement card within 24 to 48 hours.

Conclude Service

What must the customer do—for example, clean, exit, and/or stay current—to conclude the process of obtaining service and/or its benefits in a successful manner?

The actions that a customer may have to take to conclude service vary by the type of service. With services in which the customer is physically present during service delivery, concluding the service may require exit from the location and other actions, such as deplaning and retrieving luggage (when taking a flight) or getting groceries home (when shopping at a store). With many relational services, there is also an ongoing step of maintaining preferred benefits and avoiding relational problems. For example, an insurance customer wants to stay current on services, be rewarded for desirable behaviors, and keep the lowest rates available. Assurant Health has addressed these customer needs by guaranteeing a customer's health insurance rate for two years and reducing the deductible by 10 percent every six months that the customer does not meet the deductible level.

When a customer obtains service that involves changes to tangible goods, concluding the service may include taking possession of the goods (as with auto repair) or ensuring proper cleanup (for example, following a home repair). In these instances, customers would like to limit the effort they must expend to conclude service, and they also want to limit any negative repercussions of concluding service. StubHub, an online marketplace service for people who want to buy and sell event tickets, addresses these concerns by making the concluding steps of shipping a sold ticket and receiving payment a simple and convenient process. Sellers are provided a prepaid FedEx shipping label that can be printed from home at the time the order is confirmed. The shipping label's tracking number is linked to the seller's ticket listing, and it initiates the ticket buyer's payment once the system indicates that the buyer has received the tickets.

Pay for Service

What payment actions are required of the customer to ensure success obtaining service and/or its benefits?

Most services require the customer to pay for services rendered. For many services, payment is a distinct event. This is the case, for example, when one sees a movie, takes a flight, or eats out at a restaurant. However, payment can also take place over an extended period of time, whether due to the nature of the payment plan or the relational nature of the service, as with membership or contractual services such as a health club or Internet access.

Whenever paying takes place, the customer wants to be able to quickly understand and verify the accuracy of charges, minimize the time it takes to make a payment, receive accurate billing with no surprise charges, and use a preferred payment option. Lufthansa, for example, now lets customers use the online payment service PayPal to pay for travel bookings made online. In longer-term relationships, the customer also values help with making payments, such as being given affordable payment options and reminders of when payments need to be made. Flat-rate pricing is a means of making pricing more affordable and understandable to customers. Vonage, for example, has recently introduced a flat-rate international calling plan. For a flat monthly fee, customers can make unlimited calls to 60 countries covered by the plan.

Discover Service Delivery Innovation Opportunities

Once the job of obtaining service has been defined and mapped, the next step is to uncover the outcomes that customers use to define success at each step along the way. The discussion above has provided insight into the types of outcomes that might be anticipated at the various steps. However, the full field of outcomes will not be known until customers are interviewed to uncover them. As with the core job, a company should seek to uncover outcomes related to time, variability, and output, but outcomes of obtaining service have the unique characteristic of being likely to refer to the service or the service company. The questions for uncovering outcomes discussed in Chapter 3 apply, but at each step, a company may also find it useful to put into outcome (metric) form how customers define service quality descriptors such as *reliable, responsive, available, flexible,* and *convenient.* Actually, asking customers to define *un*reliable, *un*responsive, *un*available, *in*flexible, and *in*convenient service at each step can be a very productive line of questioning.

In addition, a company will find it very effective to ask customers about the pros and cons of different ways of getting each step accomplished—which is why it is important to define the job and the outcomes broadly enough that the choice of how to get steps done is not constrained. Customers can readily speak about how different methods of accomplishing the various steps affect timing, variability, and output. For example, if customers are asked about the advantages of placing a service order via the Internet, they might say that they can more quickly submit order information. On the other hand, they might indicate that a drawback of this approach is that they are not be able to confirm with a service representative when service delivery will take place. This discussion would lead to two distinct outcomes:

- Minimize the time it takes to submit order information
- Minimize the time it takes to determine when service delivery will take place

Although the conversation that led to these two outcomes focused on a specific form of service delivery (the Internet), please note that neither outcome refers to the Internet or a service representative. By defining the steps on the job map independent of a particular delivery method, the company can capture outcomes to evaluate many different forms of service delivery—even those that have not yet been created. As always, when writing up the outcomes, the investigative team must make sure the statements meet the criteria for good outcome statements and provide the level of detail required to support the company's overall service innovation goals. A sample list of outcomes for steps in the consumption chain job of obtaining health care services is provided in Table 4-2.

Once a complete list of outcomes has been uncovered, the company should have a representative sample of service customers rate each outcome for importance and satisfaction. The outcomes should then be prioritized using the opportunity algorithm described in Chapter 1. Because the outcomes are relevant across forms of service delivery, some customers can rate the outcomes with one form in mind, and others can rate the outcomes with another form in mind. For example, some customers could rate the outcomes for online service delivery, and other customers could rate the same outcomes for interpersonal service delivery. The outcome priorities can also be compared across customer segments and competitive services. In addition, any emotional jobs (see Chapter 2) related specifi-

Table 4-2 Sample Outcomes for the Job of Obtaining Health Care Services

Universal Job Step	Health Care Job Step	Outcome
Contact service provider and/or access service	Schedule health care services; go to appointment	• Increase the likelihood that a desired appointment time is available, e.g., a preferred time of day or a preferred day of the week • Minimize the amount of time spent waiting to see the provider
Define and/or communicate service needs	Explain the health problem; undergo tests	• Minimize the likelihood of forgetting to tell the provider something important about the problem • Minimize the amount of pain incurred when having a test done
Evaluate and/or select service options	Obtain a diagnosis; evaluate treatment options	• Minimize the amount of time spent waiting for a diagnosis • Minimize the time it takes to learn what treatment options are available
Confirm and/or finalize service plan	Agree to a treatment plan	• Minimize the time it takes to learn what will be required to implement the treatment plan, e.g., what medications or when therapy begins
Initiate service delivery	Obtain medical supplies	• Minimize the time it takes to figure out where to get the supplies needed to treat the problem

(continued)

Table 4-2   Sample Outcomes for the Job of Obtaining Health Care Services *(continued)*

Universal Job Step	Health Care Job Step	Outcome
Fulfill customer responsibilities	Implement the treatment plan	• Minimize the time it takes to execute the treatment routine, e.g., take medications or change dressings
Receive service	Obtain treatment	• Minimize the time it takes for the symptoms to go away, e.g., swelling, blurry vision, bleeding, or headaches • Minimize the likelihood that the health problem will return after the treatment plan is completed
Evaluate and/or monitor service delivery	Verify the effectiveness of the treatment	• Minimize the time it takes to know that the health problem has been fixed, e.g., illness is cured or injury is fixed
Adjust service plan and/or its execution	Change a treatment plan	• Minimize the time it takes to change a treatment plan that is not working
Get questions answered and/or problems resolved	Understand the problem and/or costs	• Minimize the time it takes to learn what must be done to fix the health problem • Minimize the likelihood of not knowing the cost of a test before it is done
Conclude service	Document the problem and treatment plan	• Increase the likelihood that the details of a health problem can be recalled in the future, e.g., the cause or the treatment
Pay for service	*[not part of model/afford-ability throughout]*	• Minimize the time it takes to figure out if the desired treatment plan can be afforded

cally to using a particular service can be correlated with the outcome ratings to determine which outcomes are most strongly related to which emotional jobs (see Chapter 3). For example, in the context of medical treatment, one might find that the emotional job *feel respected* is most strongly related to minimizing the time it takes to learn what is involved with each treatment option.

When we worked with Abbott Medical Optics (AMO), a leading provider of lenses and other devices for cataract and refractive surgical procedures, to discover innovation opportunities in its service delivery process, we began by interviewing materials managers about the various encounters they have with ophthalmic vendors such as AMO. We asked these customers to tell us what they were trying to accomplish in their interactions with a vendor rep, a call center employee, or other company representative. We also asked about the purpose behind other service encounters that materials managers had with AMO, including at the AMO Web site and regarding shipments and invoices. From a handful of interviews, we were able to map the process of obtaining service, which included steps such as determining lens order needs, contacting the vendor to place an order, placing an order, receiving lens replacements, reviewing and verifying orders and invoices, resolving order and billing issues, paying invoices, getting questions answered, and intermittently negotiating purchase agreements and contracts.

Next, we interviewed approximately 20 other materials managers to uncover the more than 80 outcomes they use to measure success across the range of steps in the job. We then prioritized the outcomes by having a representative sample of nearly 200 materials managers rate each outcome for importance and satisfaction.

The prioritized list of materials managers' outcomes revealed a flaw in AMO's service delivery approach. Materials managers were frustrated by ophthalmic vendors' problem resolution process, including AMO's process. They were often unsure who to contact because the issues they confronted were so various: delivery problems, lens consignment issues, and problems with invoicing and returns. AMO management recognized that delays often resulted because materials managers had to contact several people within AMO before finding someone who could help them. Matters were further complicated by the fact that the resolution of a given problem might require the involvement of several people and several layers of approval within AMO.

In response, in 2006 AMO introduced dedicated customer advocates and regional customer care teams. Customers now have a single point of contact within AMO that will help them with any issue they confront. If an issue requires additional research, an AMO advocate or member of the care team has responsibility for problem resolution, which means that customers with tricky problems no longer have to navigate opaque internal processes without a guide. Physical proximity among team members of different functional areas has also improved communication and coordination to resolve customer problems. As a result, customers' problems are resolved faster and more thoroughly. In addition, service has now assumed a more strategic role within AMO. Advocates and care team members reach out to customers on a regular basis to identify potential issues. Regional sales calls include customer care team members to ensure that everyone knows what changes are taking place. This has enabled AMO to proactively head off potential account problems and better anticipate how to grow account revenues. Since these and other changes have been introduced, AMO's Net Promoter and customer loyalty indexes have risen dramatically.[5]

Interpersonal Service Encounters

This chapter has focused on helping a company discover how customers measure success in service delivery, independent of the method of delivery. However, many services are delivered in the form of interpersonal interaction, and therefore a company can benefit from understanding how customers evaluate interpersonal service encounters, in particular. For most interpersonal service encounters, the list of criteria is not long, and they can all be captured by asking customers to describe the ideal personal encounter and what employee behaviors and attitudes they consider important. In nearly all service encounters, customers want employees to be polite, willing to help, sincere, knowledgeable, patient, caring, and enthusiastic. They want employees to instill confidence, display understanding, express concern, give them undivided attention, and know the customer's personal situation. Customers can also be asked how the ideal service encounter would make them feel. This will reveal emotional jobs such as *feel reassured, feel important, feel calm,* and *avoid feeling incompetent,* as discussed in Chapter 2.

The criteria used to evaluate interpersonal service encounters are not jobs or outcomes on obtaining service. Rather, they are feature characteristics for the interpersonal delivery of a service. Still, customers can rate these criteria and the emotional jobs for importance and satisfaction. However, the company should be sure to consider these ratings separately from those of the outcomes on obtaining service because the latter reflect how the customer measures service quality independent of how service is delivered.

SUMMARY

To receive the benefits of a service they have hired, customers must proceed through a series of steps to obtain the service. These steps provide many opportunities for a service to differentiate itself from the competition even if the core benefits it delivers are the same. The universal job map for obtaining service helps companies discover these opportunities; at each step in the job, there are unique opportunities based on how customers define success.

To assure success with service delivery innovation, a company should define the job of obtaining service broadly enough to transcend particular methods of service delivery and broadly enough to allow for the mapping of a full range of steps. Once the job has been mapped, the next step is to uncover the outcomes that customers use to define success at every step along the way. These outcomes are then ranked by opportunity, resulting in a list of promising opportunities for service delivery innovation.

CHAPTER 5

DISCOVER OPPORTUNITIES FOR SUPPLEMENTARY SERVICE INNOVATION

Product-based companies can use supplementary service innovation to help their customers get more value from the products that they are currently using to get a job done.[1] By doing so, a company can improve customer relationships, capture a larger share of revenue, differentiate itself from the competition, increase revenue stability, and, ultimately, better satisfy customer needs.[2] Supplementary service innovation is especially useful for manufacturers because it naturally complements the products they already sell. This is not to say that manufacturers shouldn't explore other forms of service innovation—the growth of IBM Global Services demonstrates that new and core service innovation hold promise for product companies too—but supplementary service innovation is a good starting point.

There are four approaches a product-based company can take for supplementary service innovation. First, it can explore supplementary service opportunities that arise from the core job that customers use its products to accomplish. Second, it can examine the consumption chain jobs that come with owning and using the company's products. Third, it can look for opportunities to improve how technical support is delivered to the customer. Fourth, it can see if there are any ways it can help the executors of related jobs get their jobs done. Let's consider each perspective in turn.

Discover Supplementary Service Innovation Opportunities Related to the Core Job

To get a given job done, customers may use both products and services. As such, the customer job provides the focal point to guide the innovation of not only next-generation products but also services that complement product capabilities. In fact, the optimal solution is often a combination of product and service, working together. Recognizing that fact, the agricultural equipment manufacturer John Deere combined product and service to help farmers with jobs such as tilling, seeding, spraying, and harvesting a field. John Deere tractors are equipped to respond to a GPS signal, obtained through a service subscription, which enables them to more accurately complete the various jobs related to farming. The technology and service combination enables hands-free equipment steering that maintains a parallel path with as little as 2 centimeters of overlap. These innovations increase profitability by helping the farmer to increase yield, complete faster passes, and reduce fuel, seed, and chemical costs.

In a similar manner, the ClearPlay DVD player illustrates the value of technology and services working together to help the customer get a core job done. Targeting families and the job of watching a movie, the DVD player relies on filters that are created on a movie-by-movie basis to eliminate unwanted profanity, excessive violence, and nudity from the movie watching experience based on the preferences of the individual. An annual service membership provides unlimited access to filters for new movie releases that can be quickly downloaded from the Internet.

As these illustrations show, products often are limited in their ability to satisfy the range of outcomes that customers need to achieve when they are doing a job. One has only to think of the many steps required to get a job done to recognize how unlikely it is that a product, on its own, will be able to help with all of them. That's where services come in. Services are especially suited to helping the customer accomplish the steps that precede the execution step in the universal job map in Chapter 3. These include defining what the job requires, locating inputs, and preparation. The same is true for some of the steps that follow the execution step, including monitoring and resolving problems with execution.

When a product partners with a service, its capabilities are expanded in a way that helps the customer to get more of the job done. The combination of product and service enabled the Nike+iPod Sport Kit to deliver added value to runners doing the job of completing a workout. A sensor placed in Nike shoes communicates with an iPod (or iPhone) being worn by the runner, providing instant audio feedback about time, distance, pace, and calories burned. The Nike+ system synchronizes workout data at nikeplus.com, where the runner can go to analyze an individual run, track progress against predefined goals, and set new performance goals. These latter tasks, in particular, are steps in the overall job that the service component of the Nike+ system helps the customer get done.

Advances in information and communications technology have made it easier than ever to combine products and services to help customers get an entire job done. Of course, a company can also introduce stand-alone services and support that help the customer accomplish other steps in the customer job. For example, H&R Block offers audit support for any individual or business that files a tax return using H&R Block's TaxCut software. In the event of an audit, H&R Block assists the tax filer with communications with the IRS, offers guidance on how to prepare for the audit, and provides in-person representation during the audit. Similarly, the DePuy family of companies offers a variety of support resources related to their surgical products to help surgeons with the entire job of treating patients. DePuy Spine, for example, offers educational brochures to help a surgeon manage patient expectations regarding the implantation of a DePuy Charité Artificial Disc.

There are at least two lessons we can learn from these examples. First, a focus on the job for which a product is hired and the outcomes that customers use to evaluate success in getting the job done will naturally point to supplementary service innovation opportunities. Unlike product requirements, outcomes reflect how customers judge value independent of how the outcomes are satisfied. Second, taking a broad view of the job the customer is trying to get done by hiring a product is more likely to reveal supplementary service innovation opportunities. If service innovation is the goal, for example, it is better for DePuy to define the surgeon job as *treat the patient condition* rather than more narrowly as *replace a disc*. It is the broader job definition that its educational brochures assist with and that is more likely to reveal other service innovation opportunities.

When we worked with a leading provider of surgical equipment and supplies, for example, we studied the job of the anesthesiologist related to our client's products. However, we defined the scope of the job, defined as *administer anesthesia*, in a way that spanned complementary solutions and encompassed job steps from formulating an anesthesia plan to transferring the patient to postoperative care. For the step of formulating an anesthesia plan, the anesthesiologist had nine desired outcomes, including the following:

- Minimize the time it takes to determine surgeon requirements for patient anesthesia

- Minimize the time it takes to determine how the anesthesia plan should be adjusted based on the patient's particulars, e.g., age, allergies, or diseases
- Minimize the likelihood of developing an anesthesia plan that requires drugs that are not available at the facility

Because these outcomes do not presume a particular solution, it is possible that either a product or a service innovation could satisfy them—or both. Once a company has mapped the job for which a product is hired, following the universal job map in Chapter 3, and it has prioritized the outcomes in getting the job done, an internal development team can evaluate the opportunities to see whether product or service innovation is more appropriate, or whether a combination would work best. When 3M applied this approach in its medical device division, it discovered an opportunity to build information management capabilities into a product line focused on the job of sterilizing surgical instruments. Software that a sterilization manager loads onto a PC connects with a 3M incubator (which reads a 3M biological indicator) and automatically captures sterilization results to assist with reporting. Mary Poul, a 3M global marketing manager, has noted, "It was a great 'aha' for a team that was originally focused just on making the indicator better."[3]

Discover Supplementary Service Innovation Opportunities Related to Consumption Chain Jobs

In addition to discovering opportunities related to the core job for which a product has been hired, a company can discover supplementary service innovation opportunities by uncovering the struggles that customers have when executing a wide range of consumption chain jobs—the activities that a customer must accomplish to receive full and continuing value from a product or service.[4] The question to ask is "What jobs must customers get done to receive the value from our product?" The goal is then to discover opportunities to help the customer get one or more of these jobs done better.

Customers of most products—at least durable goods—must execute the following consumption chain jobs to receive value from them: select a product, purchase a product, install and/or deploy a product, learn how to use a product, use a product, move and/or store a product, maintain a product, upgrade and/or update a product, and dispose of a product. Specific consumption job names may vary by product category, but the general consumption process will be the same. Each of these jobs offers innovation opportunities at any point at which customers are not satisfied with their outcomes as they attempt to get the jobs done.

With a specific consumption chain job in mind, the company must first identify the relevant customer group. Especially in business-to-business settings, the product users are often distinct from those responsible for related consumption chain jobs. Next, the company should interview customers to map the job from beginning to end using the universal job map from Chapter 3 as a guide (see Figure 3-1 and Table 3-2). Although Chapter 3 focused on discovering opportunities for core service innovation, the steps in the universal job map also apply to the execution of consumption chain jobs. As with any job, the goal of mapping a consumption chain job is to document what customers must accomplish in order to have success in getting the job done.

Guided by the job map, the company should then interview customers to uncover the outcomes they use to judge success for each step in the job. As always, desired outcomes reflect customers' metrics related to time, variability, and output in getting the job done. In addition, the company can ask customers what emotional jobs they have in relation to the specific consumption chain job. Once prioritized by opportunity, the company will then be able to determine which needs should be satisfied through product innovation, service innovation, or both.

Ingersoll-Rand, a global supplier of products and services to transportation, manufacturing, commercial and residential buildings, and agricultural industries, is finding success with an innovative service offering that addresses many top opportunities related to maintaining a compressed-air system.[5] Ingersoll-Rand introduced its PackageCare service offering in March 2007, and the customer base is growing fast. Through the PackageCare fixed-cost service contract, Ingersoll-Rand takes a proactive lead in preventative maintenance of the system, replacing parts before they fail. The service contract includes 100 percent coverage of machine upkeep, repair, and parts replacement, as well as various optional benefits that the customer can choose, such as coverage of overtime costs in the event the system is down. The PackageCare service offering relies on regular maintenance visits by expert technicians, predictive diagnostic tools, and rapid, 24-hour repair service to remove the inconvenience of maintaining a compressed-air system, reduce various customer costs, and improve the operational efficiency of a compressed-air system.

To figure out how customers define success when maintaining a compressed-air system, Ingersoll-Rand conducted 18 one-on-one interviews with individuals responsible for this consumption chain job, including business owners, maintenance managers, facility managers, and plant managers. These interviews resulted in 70 desired outcomes encompassing eight job map steps related to performing preventative maintenance. The Ingersoll-Rand team also uncovered other functional and emotional jobs related to preventative maintenance. Next, Ingersoll-Rand had more than 200 individuals from various industries who were responsible for maintenance of a compressed-air system rate the outcomes, related jobs, and emotional jobs for importance and satisfaction.

The survey results revealed 22 high-opportunity outcomes. The PackageCare service offering squarely addresses more than a dozen of these opportunities, including the following:

- Minimize the likelihood that a breakdown occurs because preventative maintenance was not performed
- Minimize the cost of performing each preventative maintenance task
- Minimize the likelihood of incurring unnecessary expenses because a preventative maintenance task is being performed sooner than needed

Ingersoll-Rand realized that by helping customers avoid problems with the compressed-air system, it would benefit as much as the customers did. Ingersoll-Rand is now working on next-generation offerings to address several of the remaining outcome and related job opportunities.

Let's now consider what customers are trying to get done with each consumption chain job and how this understanding can lead to promising service innovation opportunities.

Select a Product

What opportunities exist to help the customer with selecting a product?

When selecting a product, the customer must establish criteria for evaluation (and sometimes a budget), locate product options, gather relevant information, compare the options, and ultimately make a product decision. For more complex products, the process can sometimes be overwhelming without assistance. Often, customers are not sure what to look for in a product, and they need help establishing and prioritizing purchase requirements. In a business environment, in particular, it can be difficult to understand the requirements of others and the likely impact of product options on operations, revenues, and costs.

Customers need help making the best choice for their situation, and they will value services that help them find product options that satisfy their needs, assess product strengths and weaknesses, and evaluate options relative to evaluation criteria and the requirements of the usage environment. The house paint manufacturer Behr, for example, has a free online service that helps the customers to select a color of Behr paint for painting a room. With "Paint Your Place," customers can paint the walls of a digital image of their own room with any of the colors available through ColorSmart by Behr. This enables the customer to evaluate each paint option in the use environment.

Purchase a Product

What opportunities exist to help the customer with purchasing a product?

When purchasing a product, customers must determine when they need to make the purchase and how much of the item they need. They also must locate or configure the product for purchase, evaluate purchase options, finalize purchase details (this can include negotiation and securing approval from others), confirm that the purchase can be afforded, complete the purchase transaction (including payment) and take possession of it, verify purchase fulfillment, and deal with any postpurchase problems. The purchase process can be riddled with problems that provide opportunities for service innovation, especially for large-ticket items and replenishment situations.

Customers value innovative services that create a de facto partnership between themselves and the company to ensure that the right products are available, tailor product and purchase options to their situation and budget, and provide responsive, accurate support when issues arise. Dell addresses these opportunities through its customized Dell Premier online store, which includes negotiated pricing and only those product, shipping, and payment options authorized by a business customer. Purchase is also facilitated through side-by-side comparisons of product configurations and the ability to save order forms for frequent purchases. The online store can also be integrated with a customer's procurement system, leading to time savings and faster purchase approvals; built-in reporting tools also allow the customer to track orders and invoices online.

Install and/or Deploy a Product

What opportunities exist to help the customer with installing and/or deploying a product?

When installing a product, the customer must determine how to complete the installation, gather the necessary materials and tools, prepare the materials and installation area, complete the installation, verify accuracy, and get the product ready for use. In some situations, installation is better described as "deployment." In these cases, the customer must define a deployment plan, prepare existing products and systems, prepare affected individuals, confirm deployment readiness, and integrate new products with existing systems and processes in addition to executing many of the basic installation tasks.

For more complex installations, customers definitely value services that accomplish the installation process for them, especially if this lets them reduce costs, improve efficiency, and avoid problems that might arise if they tried to complete the installation on their own. Customers who choose to go it alone can still appreciate services that help them complete the installation correctly or that offer support in the event that problems arise. With networked products, services may even facilitate some installation activities remotely. Microsoft Application Virtualization, for example, streams applications over the Internet or via a corporate network to user desktops and laptops rather than requiring the installation of applications on individual computers. In so doing, it speeds application deployment and eliminates the need to run application-to-application compatibility testing on individual computers.

Learn How to Use a Product

What opportunities exist to help the customer with learning how to use a product?

When learning to use a new product, the customer must determine what needs to be learned, gather information to support learning, process the information, accomplish the actual learning, become proficient in the product's use, stay current on knowledge, and assess the knowledge that has been acquired. The value of proper learning is especially high when there is considerable financial or personal risk associated with incorrect product use. For example, a surgeon must ensure proficiency with a new surgical tool in order to avoid potentially harmful mistakes when operating on a patient. The higher the value of learning overall, the more the customer will value support services that reduce the time it takes to become proficient and that help to avoid mistakes in use.

Customers will value services that help them create a plan for learning, access necessary information, stay engaged in the learning process, and commit knowledge to memory in a way that translates into effective product use. DePuy, for example, offers surgeon training related to use of its portfolio of products at its newly established DePuy Institute. Led by expert medical faculty, a typical course involves a combination of lectures, demonstrations, and hands-on workshops to support all levels of learning.

Use a Product

What opportunities exist to help the customer with using a product?

When using a product, a customer must access it, prepare it for use (including setup), verify that it is ready to use, use it, ensure that it is being used properly, adjust usage, and conclude use, often by turning off functions and putting it away. At this stage, customers want efficiency and convenience, as few problems as possible, and optimal results. As with learning, the higher the potential costs associated with misuse, the more the customer will value solutions that support proper use—as long as the cost of the service is less than the cost of product misuse.

With products in which the potential costs of misuse are high, services can support the customer by managing or overseeing product use. Microsoft Services offers a service that helps customers manage server use by applying best practices, processes, and templates developed over the years by Microsoft IT staff to maintain their own systems. Configuration templates, for instance, provide customers with settings that Microsoft IT uses to optimize performance and avoid problems. Other services then help customers monitor compliance once configuration settings are established. When one considers the potential costs of flawed server configurations, such as unplanned downtime, security vulnerabilities, and staff time spent troubleshooting problems, the value of the services that Microsoft Services offers can be appreciated.

Move and/or Store a Product

What opportunities exist to help the customer with moving and/or storing a product?

When moving or storing a product, the customer must determine how to properly move or store it, prepare it for transport or storage, accomplish the task without incident, and retrieve it when transport or storage is complete. Customers often need help storing or transporting valuable products to ensure that the products are kept from damage and function properly once retrieved. Storage is also an issue for products that are inventoried for use by the customer. Here, customers are concerned in particular with the costs and space requirements of storage, the availability of products, proper management of inventory, and inventory losses.

Services can help the customer by providing the information required to make good transport and/or storage decisions, by assuming some of the risks of transport and storage, or by providing the transport or storage service itself. As the world leader in gas production for industry, Air Liquide has improved both profit margins and customer loyalty by applying its technical expertise to create services that support all gas-related activities at a customer site. Even seemingly nonhazardous gases such as oxygen pose considerable storage and distribution challenges. As part of its own production process, Air Liquide has developed state-of-the-art planning, measurement, detection, quality control, and treatment methods and technologies to optimize efficiency and ensure safety in gas storage and transport. The company now offers these methods and technologies to its customers in the form of on-site customized services. For many industrial customers, Air Liquide now manages gas flows right up to the point of use.[6]

Maintain a Product

What opportunities exist to help the customer with maintaining a product?

When maintaining a product, customers must figure out when a product requires maintenance, determine what maintenance is required and how and when to complete it, gather the materials and tools required, communicate with others about the maintenance (sometimes), prepare the product for maintenance, complete the maintenance, verify that the product is functioning properly, and get the product back into service. Maintenance often offers very good opportunities for supplementary services, especially with complex products.

A company's maintenance services often include technical support or field personnel help to complete the maintenance needed to keep the product functioning properly. More generally, customers will appreciate services that inform them when maintenance is required, monitor maintenance requirements, ensure that required parts and supplies are available, reduce the time spent on maintenance, and limit productivity losses due to product failure. HP Remote Monitoring, for example, captures information on printer function, consumables usage, and printer utilization, and it shares this information with HP and with IT professionals within the client company to help clients with replenishing printing supplies and scheduling preventative maintenance.

Upgrade and/or Update a Product

What opportunities exist to help the customer with upgrading and/ or updating a product?

When upgrading a product, customers must determine when the upgrade is needed and how to proceed with it. They must gather the inputs to complete the upgrade, prepare the product to be upgraded, prepare users for the upgrade (sometimes), complete the upgrade, verify the upgrade, understand what has changed, and deal with any problems that result. Like maintenance, upgrades offer an optimal opportunity for services. This is especially true for smart products, whose upgrades can be handled via the Internet.

Customers will value services that keep the product functioning in the optimal way, reduce the time and cost of upgrading, reduce performance degradation during an upgrade, and ensure that products and product users are ready to perform once the upgrade is complete. The automatic updating capability of many software-based products certainly provides these benefits. The Apple iPhone, for example, removes the hassle of determining when updates are available, locating relevant updates, and ensuring that updates are installed properly by automatically taking care of these tasks when customers synchronize their iPhones and computers.

Dispose of a Product

What opportunities exist to help the customer with disposing of a product?

Product disposal follows much the same pattern as upgrades: customers must determine when it is time to dispose of or replace a product and how to dispose of it. Then they must gather the product for disposal, prepare the product for disposal, verify that it is ready to be disposed, dispose of it, and complete any related tasks. When product disposal poses personal, financial, or environmental risks if done incorrectly, or when the product may have some continuing value, then disposal activities take on added complexity and importance.

Customers will value services that help them decide whether and when disposal or replacement is necessary. Services can also help with preparing products for disposal when this is a complex task, such as the disposal of personal computers in a business environment. To the extent that these services not only make disposal more convenient but also help the customer to avoid disposal costs and/or recover residual value in the product, they will be highly valued. The Calphalon ReNew program, for example, makes disposal of old cookware more convenient and reduces harm to the environment at no cost to Calphalon customers. When new cookware arrives, a customer is provided a ReNew box and a prepaid FedEx mailing label for shipping old cookware to Calphalon where it can be properly recycled. Customers even receive a free gift from Calphalon for participating.

The prior discussion has focused on product consumption jobs and their role in revealing supplementary service innovation opportunities. However, supplementary service innovation opportunities can also be discovered for *service* consumption jobs, such as selecting a service, purchasing a service, and learning how to use a service. This is especially true when the service is complex and when the people who execute the jobs are different from the people who receive the benefits of the service.

Discover Supplementary Service Innovation Opportunities Related to Product Support

The third way a company can discover supplementary service innovation opportunities is by helping customers to obtain the support they need. Figure 5-1 presents a universal job map for obtaining product support. The steps in the job map should seem familiar, as the job map is similar in content and overall flow to the job map for obtaining service discussed in detail in Chapter 4. As such, the discussion here is much briefer. Note that the job map for obtaining customer support does not presume a particular form of support contact, except for the step related to receiving a support visit.

Figure 5-1 Universal Job Map for Obtaining Product Support

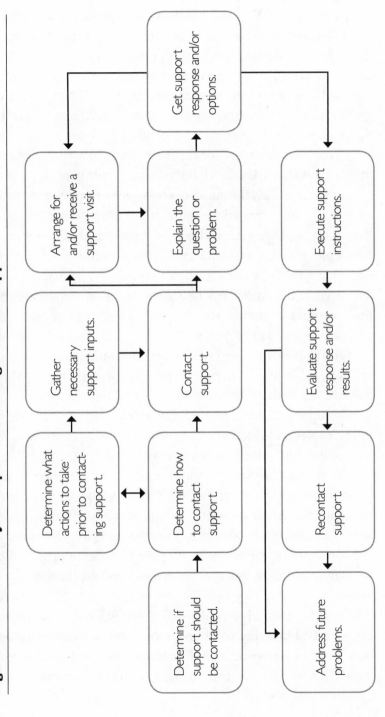

The job map in Figure 5-1 shows the process that a customer must go through to have success in obtaining product support. It begins with determining if support is necessary and how to contact the company. From there, the customer must determine what actions to take prior to contacting the company and then gather necessary inputs. Once the inputs have been collected, the customer contacts support and either explains the question or problem or arranges for a service visit, at which time the problem must be explained. If the customer only needs a question answered, then the customer must get a response to ensure job success and proceed to evaluating the support response. If the problem or question cannot be immediately dealt with or answered, then the customer must either await the field service visit or get other options for dealing with the problem, which may involve the customer's taking some action. Following this, the customer evaluates the support results and contacts the company again as necessary. (For the customer, of course, the best result is not to have to contact the company for support again.) Finally, the customer wants to ensure that he or she is prepared to address future problems of the same type.

A company can use this universal job map as the basis for interviews with customers that will reveal what outcomes they use to measure success at each step in the support job. Once these outcomes are known, the company can have them prioritized for importance and satisfaction overall, and it can have them prioritized for specific products or types of product problems. Customers can also prioritize the outcomes for forms of support contact (for example, by phone or the Internet). Table 5-1 provides illustrative outcomes for every step in the universal job map.

When Lexmark International, a leading manufacturer of printing and imaging solutions, took this approach to innovation, it conducted more than 60 consumer interviews to uncover the outcomes associated with the various consumption chain jobs related to a printer, including obtaining technical support, and to uncover the outcomes associated with printing, scanning, faxing, and copying. The outcomes were then prioritized by nearly 400 printer customers for importance and satisfaction. Through this process, Lexmark discovered that many of the top opportunities concerned obtaining technical support, and it set about making changes to improve the customer support experience. The results are leading to a mindset transformation within Lexmark: technical support is coming to be viewed as a business opportunity rather than a cost center. Lexmark is moving forward with multiple product and service innovations to make technical support more accessible to the customer. As Wade Powell, a Lexmark customer experience integration manager, has explained, "The results have enabled Lexmark to identify what the ideal customer experience ought to be and to move services and design in that direction."[7]

Table 5-1   Sample Outcomes for the Job of Obtaining Product Support

Job Step	Outcome
Determine if support should be contacted	• Increase the likelihood of being aware of a problem's requiring support before it occurs
Determine how to contact support	• Minimize the likelihood that multiple contacts with support are necessary to get different issues or problems addressed
Determine what actions to take prior to contacting support	• Minimize the time it takes to determine what steps to take to resolve an issue or problem prior to contacting support

(continued)

Job Step	Outcome
Gather necessary support inputs	• Minimize the time it takes to gather the information that support will require to address an issue or problem
Contact support	• Minimize the number of contacts that are necessary to get to a resource within the company that can address a particular issue or problem
Arrange for and/or receive a support visit	• Minimize the time it takes to get a support person to visit once the visit is scheduled
Explain the question or problem	• Minimize the likelihood that support does not understand an issue and/or problem
Get support response and/or options	• Minimize the likelihood that the recommendations are unclear, e.g., technical terminology or unclear instructions
Execute support instructions	• Minimize the time it takes to implement support recommendations
Evaluate support response and/or results	• Minimize the time it takes to determine whether support recommendations achieve the intended results
Recontact support	• Minimize the likelihood that the same information must be provided again if the company is recontacted about an issue or problem
Address future problems	• Increase the likelihood of remembering what steps to take if an issue or problem reoccurs

For example, because one of the top opportunities concerned minimizing the time it takes to determine how to contact support, Lexmark is making its contact numbers and other options more prominent in packaging and materials. At its support Web site, Lexmark has introduced new self-help documents and search capabilities to increase the likelihood that customers are able to resolve a printing problem on their own. Outcomes that customers said were important to them in their dealings with live support help included increasing the likelihood that the problem is resolved through just one interaction, minimizing the likelihood that a language barrier prevents the problem from being resolved, and minimizing the likelihood of having to repeat information to a technical support person in subsequent encounters. Armed with that knowledge, Lexmark created new agent workflows, improved the information capturing and sharing capability of its customer relationship management database, and even switched the country in which its technical support center was located to reduce language difficulties. Lexmark is also making changes to its next-generation printers to improve the technical support experience.

Discover Supplementary Service Innovation Opportunities of Related Job Executors

The final way to discover supplementary service innovation opportunities is by examining the high-opportunity needs of related job executors. A *related job executor* is a current or potential customer who has a job to do that is closely related to the core job that the company's primary customer currently hires its product to get done. Recall from Chapter 1 that multiple customer groups may rely on the services offered by a company to get a job done. The same holds true for the products a company offers.

There may be multiple customer groups who rely on the value delivered by a product or who have jobs to accomplish that are related to the products the company offers. When this is the case, the company can study the needs of these related job executors to identify product or supplementary service innovation opportunities. This can include a focus on more jobs these related job executors are trying to get done related to the product or the core job of the primary customer group, as discussed in Chapter 2. It can also include a focus on a specific core job of one or more of these related job executors, as discussed in Chapter 3.

There are three types of related job executors that should be considered, as shown in Figure 5-2: adjacent job executors, job overseers, and job beneficiaries. An *adjacent job executor* has a job to do that either operates in tandem with the core job of the primary customer or has a job to do that is linked sequentially to that core job. A nurse, for instance, works in tandem with a surgeon, who hires surgical tools to complete a surgical procedure. And so does the anesthesiologist. In a similar manner, software architects, testers, and user interface designers have roughly sequential handoffs with one another and with software developers, who hire software tools to write new code.

A *job overseer* oversees or manages the execution of the core job that the company's products or services are currently used for. Job overseers often have job titles that include the word *manager*, and many of the outcomes they use to measure successful completion of the core job relate to managing costs, waste, and overall operational efficiency. In the surgical context, for example, the manager of the operating room oversees scheduling, budgeting, staff, and surgical safety and operations for the operating room. In the software context, the project manager oversees project coordination, client management, budgeting, and project timing for the creation of a new software application. In consumer contexts, parents often act as overseers for the jobs of their children.

Figure 5-2   Job Executor Groups for Possible Service Innovation

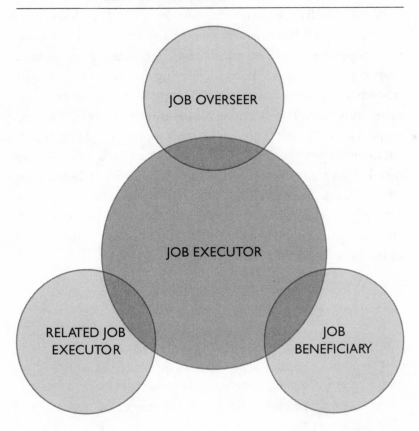

A *job beneficiary* is someone who relies on the benefits or output of the core job for which the company's products or services are used. Job beneficiaries define success with outcomes that measure how convenient it is to receive the job benefits and in terms of the overall quality of the results received. Job beneficiaries may also have their own jobs to do, jobs that relate to the output obtained from the core job. In the surgical context, the job beneficiary is the patient, who has a job to execute in relation to obtaining medical care, as described in

Chapter 4. In the software context, the job beneficiary is the user of the software being developed.

While this discussion has focused on how related job executors can help with discovering supplementary service innovation opportunities, a service company should also include related job executors when considering the different types of customers it wants to understand as it plans core or new service innovation. For example, an insurance company focused on providing benefit plans for organizations would find it useful to discover the unmet needs of both benefit managers, who develop and administer plans, and employees, who rely on benefit plans for managing their health. Similarly, a company that helps financial brokers deliver investment services to their clients would find it worthwhile to discover the unmet needs of the brokers and the brokers' clients.

SUMMARY

Product companies in particular can benefit from looking for opportunities for service innovation to support or complement their current product offerings. This chapter covered four approaches to discovering these opportunities. First, a company can look for opportunities to provide supplementary services to the customers who are currently using its products to get a core job done. Looking at the outcomes that customers use to judge success in doing the core job will reveal many opportunities that the company's products alone cannot satisfy. Second, a company can look for service innovation opportunities by investigating the consumption chain jobs customers must get done related to owning and using a product.

Third, a company can look for ways to improve how product support services are delivered. This chapter introduced a universal job map for obtaining support that can guide a company in its search for these opportunities. Finally, a company can look at the jobs that related job executors (adjacent job executors, job overseers, and job beneficiaries) are trying to get done and see if there are opportunities for service innovation there. Even if a company already has supplementary services in place related to each of these approaches, the opportunities discovered can lead to entirely new or improved services that complement current product offerings.

DISCOVER OPPORTUNITIES FOR SERVICE DELIVERY INNOVATION: THE PROVIDER PERSPECTIVE

Service innovation is about discovering opportunities to improve not only what you do but also how you do it. The preceding chapters have focused on discovering service innovation opportunities by looking at jobs from a customer perspective. However, when you are designing or redesigning how you deliver a service, you also have to think about what it takes to deliver quality service in a profitable manner. Company and employee needs must be balanced with customer needs.

The unique characteristics of services also make it challenging to deliver consistent, high-quality service: services are essentially intangible; services are often produced and consumed at the same time; services cannot be inventoried; quality control is difficult because many services involve employees and customers as part of the service. In addition to being part of the service, employees are also internal customers: they themselves rely on solutions provided by the company to get their job—the job of providing service—done. This is why it is critical to consider their perspective when determining how a service should be improved.

This chapter introduces a universal job map for service provision that a company can use to systematically discover innovation opportunities from an internal perspective. Using this universal job map, a company can identify what it must do to achieve success at every step in the process of providing service, and it can anticipate and deal with points where things could go wrong.

The Universal Job Map for Providing Service

The best service concept in the world is worth little if the company is unable to deliver on its promises in a profitable manner. In many services, the employees—both those who interact directly with customers and those working behind the scenes to support them—are the means by which the company fulfills those service promises.[1] The company's role is, first, to provide the support systems, technology, and processes that enable employees to deliver on the service promise and, second, to avoid creating hindrances and disincentives to exceptional service. The systems, technology, and processes are essentially the solutions that the company's employees hire to do the job *provide service to customers*. If these internal customers are able to do their job better, then external customers will benefit as well.

Because they are part of the service, service providers' struggles and inefficiencies often translate directly into problems and delays for external customers. The company can create exceptional value by systematically discovering and exploiting any opportunities to address those struggles and inefficiencies. This is true even when the value-adding mechanisms are not visible to the customer. For example, an information system that notifies a surgeon of a possible drug interaction with a patient prescription helps the surgeon with the crucial task of avoiding the prescription of a drug that might harm the patient—which is obviously of great benefit to the patient too, even though the patient may not be aware that the information system is in use.

The first step in discovering opportunities for service delivery innovation from an internal perspective is to define the job that service providers are trying to get done.[2] The job should be defined in a manner that parallels the job of obtaining service from the customer perspective, as discussed in Chapter 4. The focus can be either a primary service or a subservice (for example, either *sell a car* or *provide financing*; either *provide medical care* or *provide a diagnosis*).

The job does not have to be defined in a way that limits service provision to just one service provider. On the contrary, it is useful to define the job in a manner that transcends different service providers because handoffs among service providers—whether employees or service partners—are often a source of delays and problems. As discussed in past chapters, it is better to define the job broadly rather than narrowly and in a manner that is independent of how service is delivered today. Doing so opens up the innovation options available to the company.

Once the provider job is defined, it is time to map the steps involved in doing that job. The universal job map for providing service is presented in Figure 6-1. As before, this universal job map builds from the foundation of the core job map presented in Chapter 3, but it is tailored to the job of providing service. This enables greater specificity in the steps, but, as was the case with the obtaining service job map, it is likely that some steps will not be relevant to some services.

As shown in Figure 6-1, the job of providing service begins with receiving contact from the customer and ends with one or more activities to conclude the service. In between, the job of providing service requires the service provider to take steps that parallel or support the steps that the customer takes in the

Figure 6-1 Universal Job Map for Providing Service

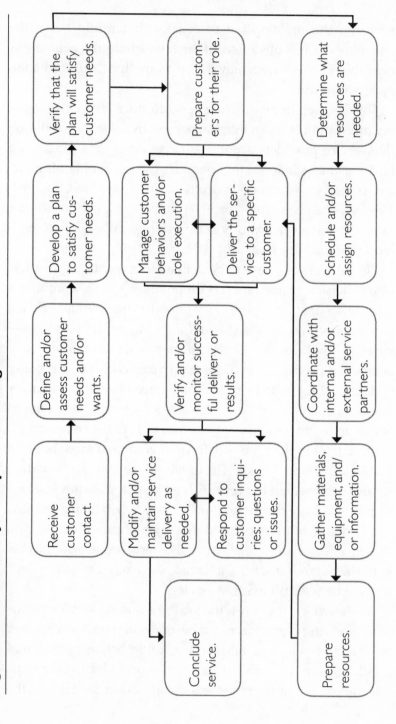

job of obtaining service (see Figure 4-1). Among the parallel steps, the service provider must define or assess customer needs, develop a plan to satisfy customer needs, verify the plan, prepare customers for their role, manage customer behavior, deliver the service, verify or monitor service delivery, modify or maintain service delivery, and respond to customer inquiries. The parallels between the customer and provider job maps emphasize the fact that success for the customer depends on success for the service provider, and vice versa. However, it does not mean that all parallel steps happen concurrently or that the provider steps occur in the presence of the customer, though they may. Also, as with the job map for obtaining service, the job map for providing service is primarily applicable to services in which the customer and the service provider interact—though interpersonal interaction is not required.

In addition, Figure 6-1 shows that the provider must execute a handful of other steps that link the verified plan and service delivery, including determining resource needs, scheduling or assigning resources, coordinating with service partners, gathering everything that is required for service delivery, and preparing those resources for service delivery. Usually, though not always, these activities are done outside the view of the customer.

As before, it is important to remember that the job map is not a blueprint of how service is delivered, though it can be used as a guide to creating a service blueprint. Rather, it is a visual depiction of what must happen in order for service to be delivered. It depicts the purposes behind various encounters with customers and other behind-the-scenes activities so that the ideal can be defined and utilized as a guide to discovering service delivery innovation opportunities. If one combines the job map for obtaining service (Figure 4-1) with the one for providing service (Figure 6-1), one gains a complete view of what must happen for successful service delivery to occur.

Guided by the framework in Figure 6-1, a company knows what steps to look for when mapping the job of providing service. If employees are central to service delivery, then one or more employee groups can be interviewed to map the job from their perspective. A summary of questions used to create the job map is presented in Table 6-1.

Once completed, the job map also provides the framework for uncovering the outcomes that service providers use to define success at every step along the way, which, as described earlier, the company can then prioritize. In this way, the company gains a complete view of what it takes to successfully deliver service to the customer from beginning to end, and it identifies where the key struggles in getting this done lie.

More broadly, the company must ensure that service delivery satisfies customer needs at appropriate quality and cost levels regardless of whether the service is delivered by employees or technology. Fortunately, even when service is delivered primarily by technology, the universal job map in Figure 6-1 is a useful guide because it breaks down the process of providing service and reveals potential inefficiencies, bottlenecks, and fail points. For example, consider the job of providing a cash withdrawal from an ATM. The ATM must identify the customer (receive customer contact), determine how much and from which account the customer wants to withdraw (assess needs), verify the withdrawal amount (develop and/or verify the plan), determine what bill denominations to collect (determine and/or schedule resources), share withdrawal information with other systems (coordinate with partners), collect the money (gather materials), get the money to the customer (prepare resources and/or deliver service), ensure that the customer knows how to use the service (prepare the customer), ensure that the customer takes the money (manage customer behavior), verify that the transaction is complete (verify successful delivery), provide another withdrawal if needed (modify service delivery), and provide a receipt if desired (conclude

Table 6-1   Questions Used to Map the Job of Providing Service

To find ways to innovate, deconstruct the job of providing service from a service employee and/or service 'overseer' perspective. By working through the questions here, you can map the job of providing service in just a handful of interviews with those inside the company who are responsible for service delivery.

Like a core job, you can start by understanding the core service delivery step, to establish context and a frame of reference. However, for this job, it may be preferable to start at the beginning of the job map and work your way through each of the steps, to define what each means for your service.

To ensure that you are mapping job steps (what the employee or overseer is trying to accomplish) rather than process solutions (what is currently being done), ask yourself the validating questions at each step.

Validating Questions

As defined, does the step specify what must be accomplished to provide service, or is it only being done to accomplish a more fundamental goal?

Valid step.   Coordinate the care plan for the patient.
Invalid step. Meet with fellow care providers.

Does the step apply universally for any provider responsible for this part of the service, or does it depend on how a particular provider does the job?

Valid step.   Determine client financial objectives.
Invalid step. Get the client to complete an assessment survey.

Defining Predelivery Steps

What must happen before service is delivered to ensure success providing service?

- What contact or identifying information must be received from the customer?

(continued)

**Table 6-1   Questions Used to Map the Job of
Providing Service** (*continued*)

- What service needs or wants of the customer must be defined or assessed?
- What must be planned or decided by the service provider to ensure success in providing service?
- What service plans or decisions must be verified or confirmed?
- What resources must be planned or selected?
- What resources must be scheduled or assigned?
- What coordination among service partners or systems is required?
- What inputs must be gathered or located?
- What resource preparation is required?
- What preparation is required of or by the customer?
- **Validate the steps.**

Defining the Service Delivery Steps

What must happen as part of service delivery to ensure success providing service?

- What responsibilities of the customer must be managed or assured?
- What service or contacts must be provided to the customer?
- **Validate the steps.**

Defining Postdelivery Steps

What must happen after service is delivered to ensure success providing service?

- What must be monitored or verified to ensure successful service results?
- What modifications or ongoing maintenance are required during or after service delivery?
- What questions or issues related to service delivery must the service provider address?
- What must be done to consider service delivery complete and to ensure success?
- **Validate the steps.**

service). Of course, it would also be good if it were possible to answer customer questions if they arise.[3]

Now let us look at the steps on the universal job map for service provision. As was true for the other universal job maps, the steps for a specific service may have somewhat different labels from those shown in Figure 6-1, and you may find that there are multiple steps for a given universal step, that the steps flow in a slightly different order, or that some steps are better combined because they happen concurrently. By referring to Figure 6-1 and the questions in Table 6-1, however, you can be sure not to miss any key steps.[4]

To illustrate the power of taking such a systematic view of what must happen to provide service, the following discussion emphasizes the unique challenges and concerns from a provider perspective—sometimes aligned with the customer perspective and sometimes not. In addition, the specific illustrations focus on what it takes to deliver efficient and effective service at each step from a provider perspective.

Receive Customer Contact

What contact or identifying information must be received from the customer to ensure success providing service?

Whether service is provided in person, remotely, or via self-service technology, customer contact with or access to the service must be managed somehow. Managing customer contact includes facilitating access not only to the overall service but also to specific locations and providers within the service. In addition, many services, such as medical care or financial services, require that customer's personal information or identity be known or verified before proceeding.

The service provider wants to get the customer to the right point of contact as efficiently as possible while still ensuring that customer needs are satisfied. In addition, the service provider wants to make a positive first impression, which means making sure that service facilities and employees convey the right image and direct the customer to the proper location. Aligning supply and demand is a key challenge at this step. If too many customers arrive at once and cannot be served in a timely manner, they are not happy. If too few customers arrive during a particular period, then the service provider may have wasted resources. To address these challenges, service providers rely on strategies to adjust or smooth demand (for example, varied pricing, self-service, reservations and/or appointments, waiting) or strategies to create flexible supply (for example, part-time help, employee cross-training, self-service, partnerships).[5] USAA, a provider of insurance and financial services to military families, manages both the supply and demand components by providing a variety of remote, self-service options to its members. This includes online banking and investing, mobile texting for account balances, and, most recently, remote check depositing by sending a photo of a paycheck using a USAA iPhone application.

Define and/or Assess Customer Needs and/or Wants

What service needs must be defined or assessed by the service provider to ensure success providing service?

To provide the service specific customers need or want, the service provider must understand their individual requirements for service delivery. This often involves soliciting inputs from the customer via one form of communication or another, but the service provider may obtain the information in other ways as well. For example, an anesthesiologist reviews medical records, patient history, and surgical case notes to determine patient anesthesia needs. A financial planner may gather a variety of inputs from clients but will also review various documents to assess customer needs. Even with very basic services, the service provider must assess individual customer needs. This may be as simple as a server in a restaurant taking a patron's order.

The goals of the customer and service provider are well aligned at this step. Both want the provider to understand all relevant customer needs as efficiently as possible. With business services, relevant needs include those related to why the service is being hired and also organizational factors that may impact success. The service provider benefits from standardized processes (for example, need assessment surveys, clear options); supporting technology (for example, medical records database, automotive diagnostics); and skills development to ensure that all relevant customer needs are understood. Doing so is key to avoiding rework and dissatisfied customers—or even harm to customers with services such as medical care. To ensure that its customers get the right amount of homeowner's insurance, for example, Chubb maintains a staff of professional home appraisers. Rather than relying on basic insurance or market valuations, a Chubb appraiser visits the customer's home and determines what it would take to rebuild it with similar-quality materials and craftsmanship. This is especially important for the custom homes that Chubb insures, and it explains why Chubb appraisers have expertise in a variety of fields, including architecture, design, and historic preservation.

Develop a Plan to Satisfy Customer Needs

What must be planned and/or decided by the service provider to ensure success providing service?

For services in which the service provider merely receives orders from the customer, the service plan and the defining of customer needs may go hand in hand. Even for these simple services, however, the provider must still decide how to fulfill the customer's requests. In more complex services, the service provider may develop a service plan that is tailored to the customer (and possibly to the customer's business environment), and doing so may require gathering information on specific service options. This is the case, for instance, when teachers put together a course plan or when financial planners develop a financial plan.

Especially with more complex services, the objective is to balance thoroughness and accuracy in the plan with efficiency in putting it together. The ideal is to develop a plan that is well suited to the customer's needs and personal situation, but efficiency argues for drawing from as few distinct information sources as possible in doing so. When employees are involved, services benefit from a combination of generalist and specialist expertise, possibly in a team structure. In general, the ability to quickly offer a customer a customized solution is of considerable value to both the provider and the customer. Carmichael Training Systems of Colorado Springs, Colorado, for example, makes it possible for its coaches to quickly develop customized training programs for individual athletes by maintaining a database of over 5,000 training programs written by the founder, Chris Carmichael, and other premier coaches. Coaches are able to select from this wealth of existing training programs and then make subtle adjustments to the plan based on individual client physiology.[6]

Verify That the Plan Will Satisfy Customer Needs

What service plans or decisions must be verified by the service provider to ensure success providing service?

The service provider can verify that a service plan will meet customer needs either with or without customer involvement. In some situations, the service provider is in a position of expertise and can make the assessment without involving the customer. For example, a pharmacist verifies the content of a prescription to ensure that there are no errors and that no harm will come to the patient; the pharmacist does this without the customer's involvement. But many services require the customer to verify the service plan. This can be as simple as verifying the content of an order or repair request or as complex as working with the provider to verify the plan for a Web redesign or consulting engagement.

Often, the service provider also needs to gain customer understanding and buy-in at this stage. With more complex services, this can be quite a challenge: the service provider must make sure that the customer understands the pros and cons of the proposal or options. In addition, this is often an important time for the service provider to answer client questions, overcome client resistance, and solicit and incorporate customer feedback to a proposed service plan—any of which can be aided not only by training systems but also by various technology and support aids. CVS added value at this step by improving the information system into which customer prescriptions were input. The original system verified the appropriateness of a drug for a particular patient and also that the prescription followed the rules set forth by a third-party payer. The problem was that data entry and verification took place after the customer had already left the pharmacy, which led to a variety of problems that required extra work on the part of the pharmacy staff. Even worse, customers became aware of some problems only when they returned to the pharmacy and their prescription had not been filled. To address this failing, CVS reordered its process so that initial data entry took place at drop-off. It embedded the change into the software used to guide the prescription-filling process to ensure consistency and compliance with the new process. The new process and supporting technology allowed pharmacy staff to resolve discrepancies while the customer was still in the store, leading to fewer fulfillment problems and greater customer satisfaction.[7]

Determine What Resources Are Needed

What resources must be planned or selected to ensure success providing service?

Once a plan is established—or as part of the plan—the service provider must determine what resources are needed to deliver the service, whether people, materials, equipment, or information. In some services, resource planning is required not only for the overall service but also for service delivery to each customer. For example, a company that builds custom homes must bring together resources that include subcontractors, backhoes, and building materials, and it must do so for each individual customer. In a similar manner, a financial planner must choose specific investment options to fulfill the plan for a given client.

The objective at this step is to ensure that all required resources are known and aligned with the plan. With customized service delivery, this is challenging because it can vary by customer. For the company as a whole, it can also be challenging because variable demand makes it hard to anticipate resource needs. Insufficient supply leads to poor service and possibly lost revenues. However, excess supply leads to wasted resources or inefficient resource use. The company benefits from processes and technologies that make it possible to deliver just enough resources to satisfy customer needs and no more. Consider how some roofing contractors are using technology to improve the efficiency of estimating resource needs when repairing or replacing a roof. Rather than relying on measurements taken at the property, Bloomfield Construction in Bloomfield, Michigan, now relies on specialized software that incorporates satellite images to remotely measure a roof and even supply materials lists. The software saves the company from having to make repeat visits to the location while still providing accurate estimates that reduce wasted materials.[8]

Schedule and/or Assign Resources

What resources must be scheduled or assigned to ensure success providing service?

In addition to planning overall resource needs, individual resources must be scheduled or assigned according to service demand and the needs of individual customers. Resources must be assigned based on who will need them and when and where they will be needed. The goal is to align resources with customer priorities and needs. There are a number of ways this can be accomplished, including giving preferred priority to some customers or assigning resources based on their suitability to individual customer needs. An auto repair service adviser, for example, prioritizes vehicles in the repair queue and assigns the workload of individual mechanics based on anticipated repair needs and the expertise of available staff.

It can be especially challenging to assign service providers to individual customers. Failure can result in dissatisfied customers and waste due to rework, delays, and unused employee capacity. Knowledge of customer needs and employee capabilities is the key to efficiently matching service providers and customers. This knowledge may reside in an individual or in some manner of information technology resource. In retail banking, for example, HSBC has dedicated specialists within each branch who are qualified to handle inquiries related to a broad spectrum of financial products, including loans, credit cards, and mortgages. However, HSBC needed an efficient way to get customers with questions about financial products to the right staff and out of the queue for banking transactions such as deposits and withdrawals. Enter Matchmaker by Qm Group. When customers arrive at the branch, a greeter determines why they are there and helps to enter their information into the Matchmaker queue management system. The system already includes all of the qualifications of staff and their areas of expertise. The system then determines the availability of staff with the appropriate qualifications, assigns a specific adviser, and informs the customers of the expected waiting time. The system also alerts the adviser to the customer's requirements.[9]

Coordinate with Internal and/or External Service Partners

What coordination among service partners or systems is required to ensure success providing service?

It's the rare service that doesn't require multiple individuals to work together to satisfy customer needs. Some work directly with the customer; others work behind the scenes. This brings the element of coordination into the picture. When multiple individuals are required to serve the customer, success depends on each individual's understanding his or her role—what it is, when it occurs, and so on. This is challenging because service delivery is often unpredictable and dynamic. In health care, for example, service providers from administrative staff to surgeons work with unpredictable schedules, dynamic patient information, and even customers who are physically moved around the service facility.

To facilitate coordination, the company must provide systems and processes that ensure that all service providers are kept up-to-date on relevant information for implementing the service delivery plan. The ideal system will ensure that all relevant information is shared with those who need it in a timely and efficient manner, and it will facilitate coordination across service partners. The Mayo Clinic, for example, has distinguished itself with a team approach to medical care. Teams are assembled to provide care for individual cases and then separated and reconfigured to care for other patients. To support this collaborative approach, the Mayo Clinic has developed not only the required service culture but also a variety of supportive technologies, including electronic patient medical records that all care providers can access and sophisticated communication technology that enables physicians to communicate with one another quickly—even remotely. The physical facility is also designed to support collaboration: hallways outside exam rooms are wide enough to allow impromptu meetings among physicians. Finally, the Mayo Clinic has removed economic disincentives to collaboration through salary compensation for physicians.[10]

Gather Materials, Equipment, and/or Information

What inputs must be gathered or located to ensure success providing service?

Materials, equipment, and information often must be brought together to fulfill the service plan. A restaurant waiter must gather together all the food a customer has ordered and bring it to the table. A pharmacist must gather drugs to fill a prescription. A teacher must locate examples and exercises to drive home learning objectives. To be successful, a company must ensure that the right, high-quality inputs are available to service providers when and where they are required to fulfill the service delivery plan. In addition, the company must help service providers to make appropriate choices among material, equipment, and information options based on service needs.

In the market research industry, one key information input for delivering service comes from respondents who complete surveys fielded on the client's behalf. Unfortunately, there is evidence to suggest that up to 29 percent of the respondents in a typical online survey may be fraudulent or unreliable.[11] To ensure that only quality inputs are captured as part of providing service to its clients, MarketTools, which undertakes surveys for clients, introduced TrueSample. Billed as the market research industry's first quality-assured sample, TrueSample validates the identity of prospective panel respondents to ensure that they are who they say they are, it relies on a digital fingerprint of a survey taker's computer to ensure that each respondent in a sample is unique, and it uses proprietary validation technology to identify and remove fraudulent respondents from the sample (for example, those who go too fast or those who don't have sufficient response variability).

Prepare Resources

What resources—for example, people, materials, equipment, and/or information—must be prepared to ensure success providing service?

After being gathered, resources often require additional preparation before service can be delivered to the customer. Materials might require organization. Equipment might require setup. Information might require evaluation or sorting. If possible, the company should consider if materials, equipment, and information can be gathered in preprepared form or at least prepared as much as possible beforehand—possibly by employees working behind the scenes. In general, preparation of employees for their role in service delivery requires that they know what is expected of them, be motivated to perform as expected, and have the skills and abilities required to succeed.

This step is often unobserved by the customer, but that doesn't mean that preparation quality should be sacrificed. On the contrary: the more critical the resource, the more important it is that methods and controls are put in place to ensure that preparation is aligned with service delivery needs. SecurAmerica pays special attention to preparing its security officers for each new assignment, for example. Before they are assigned to a client location, officers go through a two-day training program that emphasizes officer skills and client-specific service and security needs. Structured on-the-job training reinforces these skills and ensures excellence in practice. SecurAmerica also provides specialized and ongoing training to satisfy other client objectives.

Prepare Customers for Their Role

What preparation is required of or by the customer to ensure success providing service?

One vital resource that service firms sometimes overlook is the customer. At the very least, customers receive service, and it behooves the service firm to make sure the customers have reasonable expectations for what will happen before, during, and after service delivery. Beyond this, however, sometimes customers themselves play a role in service delivery. For example, a debt management counseling service relies on customers to prepare a budget and track spending—and to adjust their spending patterns.

When customers have a role in service delivery, the company must view them as partial employees and make sure that, like other employees, they know what is expected of them, are motivated to perform their role, and have the knowledge and skills required to succeed.[12] Solutions to facilitate these goals include customer selection processes, training and education, and even alignment of incentives and rewards. Charles Schwab, for example, offers various types of education to its customers to ensure that they possess the knowledge and skills required to make good investment decisions.[13] Schwab offers seminars in its branch offices that are focused on investing basics as well as self-paced educational materials to build customer knowledge and skills related to specific investment topics. For more sophisticated investors, Schwab also serves as a conduit for third-party investment reports.

Manage Customer Behaviors and/or Role Execution

What responsibilities of the customer must be managed or assured to ensure success providing service?

Just as employees must be prepared for their role *and* managed during service delivery to ensure follow-through, so must customers. Thus, it is useful to separate these steps in the service delivery process. To ensure success, the company must anticipate and understand possible failure points in customer performance and manage customer behavior to help prevent these failures.[14] In addition, employees must be capable of handling problematic customer behaviors.

The cost of managing customer behavior is balanced by the value that fewer customer failures can add—which is often substantial. Customer performance—like employee performance—can benefit from carefully designed roles, facility design, technological support, and effective leadership and communications from the company and employees. To keep patients engaged in managing their own health care, for example, Cleveland Clinic offers MyChart. Drawing on information from the electronic medical record system at Cleveland Clinic, MyChart allows patients 24-hour access to their medical information and to educational materials about their specific health issues. Using MyChart, a patient can view test results and current medications, request prescription renewals, and receive important reminders regarding preventative health tests.

Deliver the Service to a Specific Customer

What service or contacts must be provided to the customer to ensure success providing service?

This step may go by many different names depending on the service. For auto repair, it may be *deliver a repaired vehicle*. For a commercial loan, it may be *deliver funds*. For a hotel, it may be *provide a room*. The company should keep in mind what outcomes it must satisfy (in terms of time, variability, and output) in providing the service, and it must prioritize those outcomes relative to its own strategy. The ultimate goal remains to deliver a service that is differentiated in a meaningful way but that is still profitable. In addition, if employees are part of service delivery, consideration must be given to meeting the interpersonal needs of customers, such as courtesy and empathy. If the customer is physically present during service delivery, it must also ensure that the service facility "performs" as expected.

Beyond the individual service encounter, the company must ensure consistent, high-quality service delivery over time. The company must limit the number of surprises that might increase costs or cause delays. Among other things, that means balancing the productivity gains that come from standardizing or simplifying service choices with the potential for added value that comes from customization or additional service options. One option is technology that standardizes personalized service. For example, a guest service database at Marriott International enables personalized service on a global basis. After individual customers enter their preferences online just once, their requests are noted in the database and honored the next time they check in. If a guest prefers extra towels, foam pillows, or even a specific newspaper, the request will be fulfilled automatically at Marriott hotels worldwide.

Verify and/or Monitor Successful Delivery or Results

What verification or monitoring is required by the service provider to ensure success providing service?

The service provider and customer goals for verifying or monitoring service delivery are very much aligned. To ensure success, both need to know as soon as possible if the service has been delivered in a manner that satisfies the customer's needs. The teacher needs to know if students understand the material. The mechanic needs to know if a repair has resolved the car's problem. In services such as auto repair, education, and medical diagnosis, quality is difficult to monitor—especially for the customer. These services can benefit from tools and standards that help verify successful service delivery and assist with demonstrating success to the customer. More broadly, the company needs to know how things are going across service encounters and customers. The company must be able to spot problematic service trends quickly in order to determine when and where changes are required.

The company also benefits from both short-term and long-term feedback and verification mechanisms to ensure quality service. Further, processes must be put in place to ensure that employees (and customers) are able and motivated to identify and correct deficient service. For example, the award-winning Robert Wood Johnson University Hospital, in Hamilton (RWJ Hamilton), New Jersey, redesigned its case management function to proactively monitor adherence to treatment guidelines it established in partnership with its medical staff. When deviations in patient care are identified, they are brought to the attention of the care team during daily rounds. This combination of established standards and proactive monitoring enables RWJ Hamilton to ensure that every patient receives exceptional medical care. In addition, systemic problems are identified through ongoing monitoring of patient outcomes, and feedback is provided to department heads or individual providers as appropriate.

Modify and/or Maintain Service Delivery as Needed

What modifications or ongoing maintenance to service are required by the service provider to ensure success providing service?

Sometimes, to be successful, service delivery requires modification. This can be due to problems encountered during service delivery, or it can be simply because of the need to make updates to ensure continued service relevance and an optimal experience. A meal must be redone if it is under- or overcooked. A financial plan must be updated based on a change in the customer's situation. The objective for both customer and service provider is to have as few modifications as possible. If all the prior steps have been done right, more than half the battle is won. Some services also require the service provider to maintain elements of service delivery or key inputs over time—for example, a bank may maintain an open credit line for a business, and a hospital will maintain patient health records.

To ensure success, the company should develop processes, technologies, and skills among service providers to deal with anticipated or frequent changes. When changes are necessary, the service provider must be prepared to make them quickly and without creating any new problems. Customers and key service partners need to be made aware and supportive of the changes. Most services can also benefit from developing the capacity to deal with changes they don't expect, as well. The Ritz-Carlton Hotel Company builds in this capability through its employee selection processes, its service standards, and a culture that encourages employee ownership of complete guest satisfaction. At least 3 of its 12 core service statements directly concern empowering employees to address guest needs: "I am always responsive to the expressed and unexpressed wishes and needs of our guests"; "I am empowered to create unique, memorable, and personal experiences for our guests"; "I own and immediately resolve guest problems."[15] That final statement is backed by hotel funds that are made available to employees to use at their discretion to satisfy the guests.

Respond to Customer Inquiries: Questions or Issues

What questions or issues related to service delivery must the service provider address to ensure success providing service?

When customers have questions or issues, the service provider must be prepared to resolve them without interrupting service delivery to others. It is tempting to view customer questions, and especially complaints, as disturbances to be controlled away. Indeed, some service companies make it very difficult for the customer to get questions answered or problems resolved. Presumably, they do this in the interest of cost savings. However, it is a shortsighted perspective. The company should offer an easy way for the customer to make inquiries and should prepare employees and systems to handle the questions and concerns that arise.

A good approach is to consider organizational structures, processes, and technologies that enable customers to get a response to their inquiries while minimizing cost and time commitment by the company. Self-service options, for example, allow customers to answer common questions in a way that is very cost-effective for the company. In general, organizational structures that separate those who deliver service from those who respond to inquiries can reduce costs because it means that service delivery can continue without interruption. Recall the example of Abbott Medical Optics (AMO) from Chapter 4. The changes that AMO made were beneficial not only from the customer's perspective but internally as well. Because AMO employees are assigned to particular client accounts, they are more efficient at understanding clients' situations when problems arise. This structure also reduces the burden on salespeople, who might otherwise be contacted about customer problems. Because care team members are located close to one another, they are able to develop coordinated responses to customer inquiries quickly. Finally, by automatically directing

AMO's top clients to a dedicated advocate, the company ensures that support costs are aligned with client value.

Conclude Service

What must the service provider do to conclude the process of providing service in a successful manner?

To conclude service, the company should consider what actions are required to ensure that all the obligations that the service entails (for example, environmental compliance, medical documentation, or payment) have been met. At what point is the service considered complete? What final actions are required to ensure that the customer receives the benefits intended? The goal for any service provider is to leave the customer with a positive last impression. Concluding the service successfully may require helping the customer to physically leave the service facility and transition to activities that naturally follow service delivery. Getting to the airport, for example, naturally follows a stay at a hotel. If customer possessions have been part of the service delivery experience, as with car repair or a journey by plane, then success requires helping the customer to retrieve them in good condition as well.

In much the way that MyChart connects the Cleveland Clinic and patients, the clinic's DrConnect program enables referring physicians to share real-time access to patient treatment information. Physicians are provided anytime access to the entire medical record of patients they have referred, and they are sent an e-mail once a day to notify them of all new patient care information. Although DrConnect provides a direct benefit to the referring physician, it can also be viewed as a critical part of concluding service delivery to the patient. To ensure that the patient receives optimal medical care after leaving the clinic, the referring physician needs a comprehensive understanding of the care that has been provided at the clinic. DrConnect enables referring physicians to base their care decisions on a complete medical history, which ultimately improves the care the patient receives.

The Service Provider Perspective

Employees who serve customers play at least two distinct roles of relevance to service innovation. First, they are internal customers of the company and other service providers. With this role in mind, it is important to map the job of providing service from the perspective of key service employee groups and to uncover the outcomes each group uses to measure success. If service employees experience delays, mistakes, and rework at any given step in the job, these will negatively impact the customer experience or at least result in inefficiency in the service system.

Second, these employees are part of the service solution that delivers value to customers. With this role in mind, it is important to include service employees—both line employees and job overseer groups—in new service concept creation, design, and development. The job overseer, you will recall from Chapter 5, represents the management or ownership interests of the company. The job overseer manages the service provided by employees and possibly the entire service delivery process. As discussed throughout this chapter, the company perspective provides valuable insight into cost, waste, and inefficiency concerns for the service as a whole. For each step in the job map, the distinct service provider groups and service overseer groups should be interviewed—separately—to uncover how they define success in providing service in terms of time, variability, and output, as discussed in Chapter 3. The final list of outcomes can then be prioritized for opportunity, as discussed in Chapter 1.[16] For the overseer group in particular, it may be valuable to rate the outcomes with different forms of service delivery in mind (for example, telephone, Internet, in person, self-service kiosk).

Each step in the job map provides an opportunity to discover ways to improve service delivery from the provider perspective. Some questions to consider at each step are:

- From an internal perspective, what are the high-opportunity outcomes related to efficiency (time outcomes), consistency (variability outcomes), and cost and results (output outcomes)?
- What would the ideal scenario look like from the perspective of the company (considering customer needs, of course)? What would the ideal scenario look like from the perspective of service employees?
- What could possibly go wrong that would detract from the service delivered to the customer? What can be done to prevent such problems?
- What actions must the company perform to deliver the service the customer needs? What must service employees and customers do?
- What system, equipment, material, information, process, and facility requirements must be met to deliver the service the customer needs? [17]

SUMMARY

This chapter has provided the final perspective required to discover service innovation opportunities—the provider perspective. To deliver on its promises to customers, a company must consider what it takes to provide efficient and effective service. By systematically mapping what must happen to provide exceptional service, a company can discover opportunities to improve its service solution at every step in the job. As part of the service delivery process, employees who serve customers provide essential insight into where innovation can improve how service is delivered.

To help companies discover these opportunities, this chapter introduced a universal job map for the job of providing service. In addition, consideration was given to the types of opportunities that companies are likely to identify at each step in the job based on what success looks like from a provider perspective. Once the job has been mapped for a specific service, the next step is to uncover the outcomes that define success from an internal perspective at every step along the way. The outcomes are then prioritized by opportunity to discover opportunities for service delivery innovation. As before, a company can follow this approach for the various distinct services it offers.

In addition to revealing service innovation opportunities from an internal perspective, the universal job map for providing service can guide the design of a current or new service to satisfy the unmet needs of customers. That element is why this chapter provides a bridge between discovering service innovation opportunities—our focus in the preceding chapters—and designing new or improved services, which we will turn to in the remaining chapters.

CHAPTER 7

DISCOVER WAYS TO DIFFERENTIATE SERVICE DELIVERY

Once customer needs have been uncovered and prioritized, it is time to develop a service strategy that is unique and valuable to customers. If the goal is to improve a current service, then each element of the current service offering must be scrutinized for its impact on customer needs and whether changes are in order. If the goal is to create a new service, then each element of the service concept must be designed to deliver customer and company value.

There are two sides to a service concept: what it provides to customers and how it does the providing. Chapter 8 will cover how both aspects come together to create a winning service concept; here we will examine a comprehensive list of service design dimensions that covers the key choices available to a company for how it delivers a service.[1] Although the possibilities for *what* a service should do are quite varied and depend on the jobs that customers are trying to get done, the primary dimensions for *how* a service is provided have been established by service scholars over the past three decades. My goal is to explain each dimension and what it means to choose one alternative over another. Armed with this knowledge, a company will make better decisions regarding how to deliver a differentiated and profitable service concept.

The Dimensions of Service Delivery

In the Introduction to this book, I argued that undue attention to the differences between goods and services has actually constrained thinking about how to approach service innovation. But I also noted that the differences between goods and services are relevant when it comes to the design (or redesign) of services. Let's consider how:

The "four P's" of the traditional marketing mix are *product, price, place,* and *promotion*. But services require something extra. With services, employees often deliver the service to customers who are physically present in the service facility, and those customers may even have a role in coproducing the service, as we saw in the last chapter. So, in addition to the original four P's, the services marketing mix includes three additional P's: *people* (employees and customers); *physical evidence* (facility, equipment, employee appearance, other tangibles); and *processes* (operating procedures, flow of activities).[2] Together, the seven P's of the services marketing mix define the elements of a service that are within the control of the firm.

Service delivery involves three interrelated organizational functions: marketing, operations, and human resources. Marketing, which focuses on customer satisfaction and revenue growth, makes decisions regarding who is served, how customer relationships are managed, how the offering is presented to customers, and how the offering is priced. Operations, which focuses on quality control, cost effectiveness, and efficiency, makes decisions regarding when, where, and how services are offered. Finally, human resources, which focuses on aligning providers with marketing and operations goals, makes decisions regarding how work is organized and how tasks are structured.

Figure 7-1 provides a summary of the primary strategic design options available for service delivery. They are grouped

Figure 7-1   Strategic Service Design Dimensions

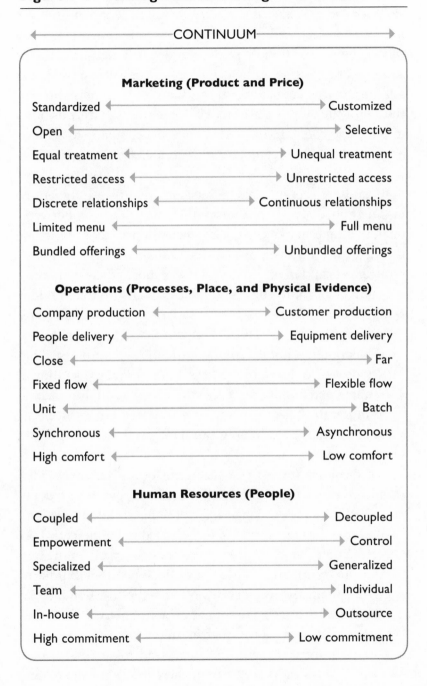

broadly according to their alignment with marketing (decisions related to *product* and *price*); operations (decisions related to *processes, place,* and *physical evidence*); and human resources (decisions related to how *people* work).[3] Although the dimensions can be considered one at a time, a company must make sure its choices are synergistic and internally consistent. It is the aggregate of the choices that becomes the service, positions it relative to competition, and enables the company to achieve a profit. As such, a company must understand the pros and cons of each choice.

It can be difficult to make decisions that please the entire organization. There may be conflicts, for example, between operations and marketing goals: whereas operations may favor reducing the number of choices available to customers to reduce costs and make service delivery more efficient, marketing may favor more customer choices to ensure that a wider range of customer needs can be satisfied. Christopher Lovelock, a founder of the field of services marketing, concluded, "The solution lies not in looking for foolish compromises that satisfy no one, but in looking for synergy among operational, marketing, and human resource strategies."[4] With the outcome priorities of the customers, the company, and the service providers in mind, the company can make well-informed trade-offs.

When conflicts arise in satisfying customers' outcomes, they should be viewed as opportunities to take a new service delivery approach that challenges conventional industry wisdom. Many breakthrough services, including the online bank ING Direct, MinuteClinic, the University of Phoenix (an online university program), and Netflix, have done just that. Similarly, over time, competitive services often come to resemble one another because they make similar choices, but a careful reconsideration of design choices with an understanding of customers' high-opportunity outcomes can lead to successful new services. This is especially true if there are segments of customers who value distinct outcomes (and cost)—that is, groups of customers with shared priorities for the trade-offs they are willing to make.[5] As the strategy guru Michael Porter has argued, trade-offs are the essence of strategy. You just want to be able to make the right ones.

The strategic design dimensions of Figure 7-1 can be applied to the overall service and also to each step in delivering service to the customer, including behind-the-scenes activities, as illustrated in Figure 7-2. The choices made across steps do not necessarily have to be the same.

For example, a consulting organization could rely almost exclusively on service providers to assess customer needs, but then it could rely on a software program (equipment) to develop a plan based on those needs. In fact, the choices made within steps do not have to be the same. A fast-food restaurant, for example, could allow customers to customize how they want their meat cooked, but not what toppings are put on a hamburger—or vice versa. For this reason, I do not categorize services by the choices on the different dimensions, although that is a common practice. A consulting organization, for example, can choose to offer standardized or customized service, to be open or selective in the customers it serves, to be specialized or generalized, and so on. Finally, note that although the dimensions are presented as choices, they actually exist on a continuum.

Standardized or Customized?

This dimension offers a choice between uniform processing of customers, things, and information (for example, set rules, codes, templates, and procedures) and flexible processing based on customers' needs or preferences. Standardized service relies on nonvarying processes and choices, though several choices may be available to the customer. Customized service, in contrast, utilizes a unique service process that is

Figure 7-2   Designing How Service Is Provided

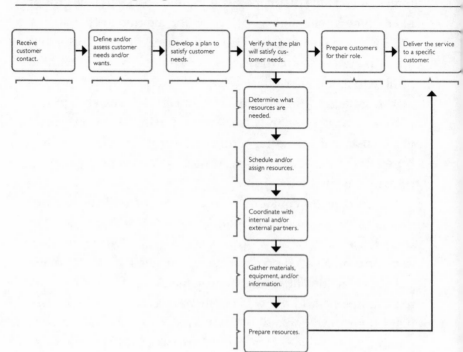

created or adapted based on each customer's situation. Whereas one hospital may have a set care plan for each patient with a particular condition, another may work with individual patients to develop a care plan that fits their lifestyle, diet preferences, and so on. Standardization is advantageous because it ensures consistency of service delivery across customers. It also supports productivity and efficiency goals. The more homogenous customer needs are, the more appropriate standardization is. Customization provides a means of satisfying the unique needs of individual customers to the fullest extent, but it can be unreliable, and it is very costly to deliver and support (for example, employee hiring, training, and compensation costs may be higher).

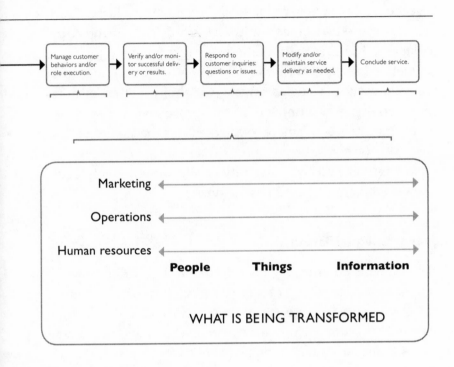

Open or Selective?

This dimension offers a choice between providing services to any and all customers and only providing services to a select group of customers. A company may decide that it only wants to provide services to some types of customers. That decision may allow it to focus its service delivery while still ensuring that customer and company needs are satisfied. Sometimes the decision may be a financial one: services may be offered only to those customers with certain revenue or profit potential. Alternatively, there may be certain types of customers who are more likely to ensure that the service will be delivered successfully, whether due to the fit between their needs and what the service does or due to their capabilities or motivation.[6] The

selection decision may be made up front (as with Curves' decision to serve only women), or it can be made on a customer-by-
customer basis with customers being evaluated for fit to
predefined selection criteria. Poor fit between customers and
what the service can deliver creates variability that undermines
productivity, and ultimately it leads to customer dissatisfac-
tion. Of course, being more selective means that some customers are not served, which translates into fewer revenue
opportunities and the possibility of alienating potential customers who are excluded from service.

Equal or Unequal Treatment?

This dimension offers a choice between giving all customers
the same level and type of service and giving some customers
special services and treatment. In some respects, the decision
taken for this dimension can be applied to all the other dimensions. Some customers could be offered a full menu of choices,
and some could be offered a limited menu. Some could be
offered customized service whereas others might be offered
only the standardized service. This is akin to the distinction
between standard and premium service—and often the distinction between standard and premium pricing. Higher costs
associated with some services demand that they be offered to
only those customers whose revenue justifies it or who are
willing to pay extra for special treatment. When special treatment comes with premium pricing, it creates an additional revenue stream. It also gives the company a way to reward
high-value clients and motivate second-tier clients to do what
it takes to receive premium-level service. When used in combination with technology, unequal treatment can be applied on
a customer-by-customer basis. The key drawback is potential
resentment among lower-tier customers if they are aware of
varying service tiers and believe the differentiation to be

unfair. To be successful, a company should consider not only current profitability but also future customer profitability.

Restricted or Unrestricted Access?

This dimension offers a choice between few or many restrictions on when, where, and how the service is made available to customers. Increasingly, many services are available 24 hours a day, 7 days a week, and 365 days a year, at least in some delivery forms (for example, telephone or the Internet). Mobile service access is also enabling some services (or some steps in the service delivery process) to be accessed wherever the customer is located. The "how" element is also important: having a variety of ways to access the service makes it convenient for a broader array of customers. Of course, greater access generally comes with greater costs. For in-person service delivery, this may translate into both higher fixed and variable costs. Unrestricted access may not make sense for some companies. It makes most sense if there are customer segments that demand more unrestricted access, if the company has high fixed costs and if customers are willing to pay more for the greater freedom or if costs can otherwise be controlled. Technology, for example, can make some services available with few restrictions and limited impact on variable costs. All companies should consider which steps in service delivery would benefit most from less restricted access. In banking, for example, customers generally value flexibility in making a cash withdrawal more than flexibility in making a deposit (though USAA, discussed in Chapter 6, now provides this as well). Overall, the cost of less restricted access will be more manageable when the service delivery involves the processing of information based on simple rules rather than the processing of tangible goods.

Discrete or Continuous Relationships?

This dimension offers a choice between service delivery via one or more discrete transactions and delivery via an ongoing, connected relationship. Ongoing relationships offer customers an opportunity to learn about service operations and their own role. This gives customers greater confidence, reduced anxiety, and a greater sense of belonging. As customers learn, they are also more likely to contribute higher-quality inputs and to perform their role better, which can lead to greater efficiency and service quality. In addition, as the customer and company become more connected, the company learns more about the customer, which can lead to more efficient and effective service delivery. Beyond the service delivery benefits, the company may also benefit from increased purchases over time. Of course, a true ongoing relationship implies a company investment in creating financial, social, customization, and/or structural bonds with the customer, such as investments in information systems, employee training, and new organizational structures. These investments have both financial and operational costs, and the company must therefore consider the likely return on the investment based on customer, company, and service provider outcomes. And, if a relationship is advantageous to the company, the value must be made clear to the customer as well.

Limited or Full Menu?

This dimension offers a choice concerning the number of options made available to customers: should the company offer few, or many? There are two ways in which customers are provided more choices. First, customers may be provided a greater breadth of options for the service as a whole or for individual delivery steps, as when a restaurant has many types of cuisine or a repair shop performs many different types of repairs. Second, customers may be provided a greater depth of options. A supermarket, for example, may offer a half-dozen brands of diapers in several different package sizes, whereas Sam's Club may only offer one or two diaper brands or package sizes.

Greater breadth of options positions the service as a generalist to whom customers can come in many situations—to help them complete many different jobs. Greater depth positions the service as a specialist to whom customers can come to find help with a specific job. More choices can attract more customers, produce additional revenue opportunities for the company, and may protect against wide variation in sales. At the same time, however, they introduce complexity, which increases management and staffing costs (for instance, in the form of additional training), they may require other infrastructure (such as equipment), and they make it more difficult to match supply with demand. Because a wide range of services is likely to require specialist staff and equipment for each service area, it can lead to excess overhead. General hospitals, for example, labor under an overhead burden that specialized surgical centers can avoid. More choices should be added only when customer needs demand it and the additional choices fit with the current service delivery model and strategy.

Bundled or Unbundled Offerings?

This dimension offers a choice between bundling service offerings together and selling services separately. This could be service-with-service bundling or service-with-product bundling. Companies bundle products and services either to increase customers' perceptions of value or to simplify the purchase decision by combining complementary offerings. For the company, it is an opportunity to increase revenues. Generally, a bundling strategy is obvious, as when complementary offerings such as a product and a maintenance service are sold together or when customer education is provided free with a consulting engagement. At other times, it depends on how the company defines its service. In reality, even a single service is a bundle of subservices and tangible items. For example, a marketing research service may consist of help with planning, survey quality review, survey programming, data collection, quality control, and data analysis—any of which can be sold together as one service or individually as separate services. Many product companies throw in services for free, and their customers fail to see the value in the service. Those companies should consider selling the services separately or at least unbundling them and then discounting them so customers can appreciate their value.

Company or Customer Production?

This dimension asks the company to decide the extent to which it and the customer will be responsible for doing the work of service delivery. A full-service operation does everything for the customer. A self-service operation relies on the customer to do all the work. Most services have both full-service and self-service elements, especially across steps in the service delivery process. Whereas one restaurant expects customers to pick up their own food and clean up after themselves, another restaurant has servers to do this work. There are even restaurants at which customers cook their own food . . . and are charged more for the experience. The last example illustrates that self-service does not need to be viewed negatively. At the very least, customers may view self-service favorably due to added convenience and, sometimes, lower price. From the company perspective, customer coproduction can reduce costs, increase productivity, help align supply and demand, and facilitate customization. If customers have better access to certain required inputs, customer coproduction can also improve efficiency. However, customer coproduction introduces the challenge of managing a volunteer workforce composed of individuals with varying skill and motivation levels. The result may be service delivery bottlenecks and inconsistent quality. Relying on customers makes sense only if customers are able and willing to fulfill the desired role.

Delivery via People or Equipment?

This dimension offers the choice of delivering the service by people or equipment. It could also be called "High Touch or High Tech?" or "Manual or Automatic?" For a manual service, people do the processing of customers, things, and information. For an automatic service, equipment does the processing. Nearly all services—auto repair, medical care, banking, education, and more—are trending toward increased technology and equipment usage. In many cases, equipment is used to replace people or to provide an alternative service delivery platform that "competes" with people providing service (as is the case with Internet retailing). Automated processes provide very flexible capacity and are more efficient and less variable, and they often produce more thorough, personalized, and accurate results. They offer some of these same benefits when used in support of other tasks being done by customers or employees. Equipment, however, introduces high fixed costs and lacks the flexibility for dealing with heterogeneous customer needs, inputs, processing, and outputs—though sophisticated programming is continually narrowing this gap. Thus, automation is most appropriate for standardized processes or when the rules for customization are well defined. As always, the choice must be made not only with consideration of the company perspective in mind but also with consideration of the outcomes that customers are trying to satisfy. Some customer segments may simply prefer working with a person. In particular, inexperienced customers will be more likely to value interpersonal service delivery.

Close or Far?

This dimension offers a choice of where service delivery activities physically take place—close to the customer or far away. It could also be called "High Convenience or Low Convenience?" Even services that require the physical presence of the customer must make choices about where to locate a physical facility, and some services can even be brought to the customer (a mobile blood bank, for example). Also, there may be some steps in the service delivery process whose activities can be located closer or farther away from the customer. This decision encompasses where to physically locate services and people within a specific location as well: whereas one university might have a library located in each college, another might have only one central library to cover all colleges. With technology advances, some services that have historically required close physical proximity to the customer (for example, teaching, medical diagnosis, entertainment, banking) no longer do. Locating services closer to the customer increases the convenience for the customer, but it also increases costs for the company because rents are higher and investments in facilities and service providers may need to be duplicated.

Fixed or Flexible Flow?

This dimension offers a choice between predetermined service delivery processes or flows and ones that are adaptable based on the customer's situation or changing company objectives. With a fixed flow, customers, things, and information are processed with the same steps and in the same order each time.

With a flexible flow, the steps may not all be completed, or they may be completed in a different order on different service delivery occasions. Whether the customer is physically present or the service is provided remotely (via the Internet, for example), the layout of the service must support the desired or possible flow of activity. For example, an online travel service can allow browsing according to personal preference. However, once a travel package is selected, the customer must move through a fixed set of screens to purchase it. A fixed flow ensures that all service delivery activities are completed in the optimal sequence each time service is provided. However, it may require the completion of unnecessary activities—at least from a customer's perspective—and it is more likely to create bottlenecks. For that reason, fixed flows are most appropriate when steps should be the same regardless of the customer, object, or information being processed. This is more likely when the service inputs (including customers) are relatively homogenous. A flexible flow is more cost-effective and efficient with highly variable inputs, but it is more difficult to manage due to more unpredictable demand.

Unit or Batch Processing?

This dimension asks the company to choose whether customers, things, and information will be processed as single units or in groups. As a continuum, it can also represent consideration of the size of groups. It may seem unusual to think of the processing of customers in "batches," but it is actually common in education, fitness, and air travel. However, for each of these, there are also services that focus on the individual (for example, individual tutors, personal fitness trainers, chartered jets). And, on the other hand, many services that have traditionally served individual customers have differentiated themselves by adopting a group focus. This is the case, for example, with group taxis, family-style restaurants, and less-than-truckload shipping. Sometimes, customers who are processed in batches may feel as though they are getting less personal attention, but in other cases, being in a group is a favorable part of the experience. For customers, things, and information, batch processing is generally more cost-effective, and it makes the most efficient use of people, equipment, and facility capacity. However, batch processing can create delays because individual service delivery actions must wait until a batch is ready.

Synchronous or Asynchronous?

This dimension offers a choice between timing service delivery processes so that they are coordinated to occur at the same time (or close in time) and timing them so that they occur at very different points in time. More specifically, it asks the company to decide whether the service will be delivered at the same time as the customer's request. Customer requests and provider actions are closely coordinated in a synchronous process. Because customers provide inputs that trigger service responses at many distinct points in the process of obtaining service, there are many points at which a service process can be synchronous or asynchronous. For example, one university might teach an online class in which students are able to ask questions and get responses in real time from the professor (synchronous service delivery). Another university might allow students to submit questions, but it will provide answers only at a later point in time because the lecture is not delivered in real time (asynchronous service delivery). In addition, the service delivery process entails many provider-to-provider handoffs that the company can also choose to make either synchronous or asynchronous. Synchronous service delivery provides the benefits of real-time interaction, including fast responses and immediate feedback. Asynchronous service delivery is often less expensive, however, and gives both the customer and the service provider the time to consider and develop their responses. It also enables resources to be used more effectively because work can be done as time permits.

High Comfort or Low Comfort?

This dimension offers a choice between having the tangibles of the service offering emphasize company productivity and efficiency goals and having them emphasize the customer's comfort and other needs. The tangibles of a service include elements of the physical facility (for example, its design, colors, layout); the dress and mannerisms of staff; and the look of equipment, materials, and other physical items that are given to the customer. One restaurant might cater to customer comfort and choose to have low lighting, leather seats, and plenty of space between tables. Another restaurant might emphasize the company's own productivity and efficiency goals and choose to have bright lighting, hard plastic seating, and little space between tables. In each case, the tangibles help to convey a desired image and support operational goals. The first restaurant wants customers to feel relaxed and avoid feeling rushed in order to encourage increased spending, whereas the second restaurant wants customers to leave once they have finished eating in order to free up seating for other customers. Low-comfort services are less expensive to create and maintain. A high-comfort emphasis is more important when customers have many emotional jobs they are trying to get done (for example, *avoid feeling anxious* or *feel pampered*) in conjunction with the service. If the service is one that customers cannot easily evaluate, then the company must also provide tangible clues that let the customer know what level of service is being provided.[7]

Coupled or Decoupled?

This dimension asks companies to choose the degree to which front-office and back-office activities are separated or combined. In part, the decision will depend on how much service is delivered face to face and how much is delivered remotely. A decoupled service is one in which the only activities that are performed in the presence of the customer are those that absolutely must be. In other words, the customer spends only as much time with the service provider as necessary. Additionally, a decoupled service is one in which employees who serve customers perform only those activities that must be done in the customer's presence: they don't perform any activities that can be done in the back office. One bank might have a lender who both helps the customer apply for a loan and approves the loan (coupled), while another bank might accept loan applications at the branch and approve loans at corporate headquarters (decoupled). There has been a general preference in many service industries over the past three decades to decouple service in both of these ways. Decoupled service is considered more efficient and cost-effective because decoupled back-office activities are easier to standardize and manage for efficiency. Whenever the customer is physically present, it becomes more difficult to match supply and demand and control quality. Despite its advantages, decoupling service activities can cause total service time to increase even if individual task completion is more efficient. It can also cause coordination problems and make it harder to process special requests.[8]

Empowerment or Control?

This dimension offers a choice concerning the amount of discretion that employees will be allowed to use in providing service to customers. When employees are the means by which service is delivered, they have to rely on either their own judgment in making decisions or on the rules, processes, or authority of the company. This is the case for both front-office and back-office employees. Top-down, high-control companies provide the rules and highly structured roles. Although we tend to think of professionals as exercising their own judgment and being empowered to make changes in how things are done, this is not equally true in all environments or across all service delivery steps. For example, a physician who works for a corporate-run surgical center has considerably less discretion than a physician in private practice in order to control costs and ensure alignment with other parts of the service. Empowerment makes service delivery more responsive to special requests and unpredictable service scenarios. However, it is more costly to hire, train, and support an empowered workforce. Further, having an empowered workforce can lead to inconsistent service quality and challenges coordinating among service providers. Greater empowerment makes sense when the strategy calls for customization and when the service is nonroutine and complex; such situations benefit from the faster decision making that it makes possible.

Specialized or Generalized?

This dimension offers a choice between using highly skilled specialists and less skilled generalists to deliver service. Different levels of specialization and skill can be applied to serving customer needs at each step in the process. This includes different levels of specialization among professional service providers. For example, a tax attorney is more specialized than a general-practice lawyer, who is more skilled than a paralegal. Similarly, urologists are more specialized than primary care physicians, who are more highly skilled than nurse practitioners in diagnosing a medical condition. One medical center may decide to have patients see a physician to receive a diagnosis, while another may have patients see a nurse practitioner. Less specialized service providers have the advantage of being less expensive, and having them provide service when their skill levels are appropriate for the situation can be a good decision for companies. Very cost-effective service models have resulted from a greater reliance on less skilled generalists in combination with a selective customer focus. As the ways to satisfy complex customer needs becomes well understood, less skilled generalists are able to follow simple rules to serve customers who would previously have required specialists. However, such a model requires emphasis on serving customers with needs that are well understood. From a customer perspective, such a shift increases convenience while reducing costs and providing "good-enough" service.[9] More generally, the more heterogeneous customer needs are, the more desirable generalist knowledge is from a given employee or across employees.

Team or Individual?

This dimension offers a choice concerning whether service is delivered by a team or an individual. When multiple individuals are responsible for providing services, it asks the company to choose the degree to which these individuals work as a unit as opposed to simply as a collection of individuals. In truth, any service that requires the participation of more than one individual can benefit when all participants emphasize teamwork, but that is not the focus here. Rather, this dimension asks how, concretely speaking, the different individuals involved in service delivery are organized and rewarded. When multiple individuals are responsible for service delivery, they can have rewards that focus them on individual, perhaps conflicting, goals or have rewards tied to a common objective. They can also be organized according to functional or specialty areas or organized cross-functionally into teams focused on the customer. Depending on the issue, for example, a customer with a problem may need to contact one or more of several distinct functional areas, but if the company has adopted cross-functional teams for customer support, the customer has one contact point for any and all problems. When service delivery relies on different functional areas, a team structure provides more efficient and higher-quality service. It places the focus on the customer as opposed to the function. Teams are more challenging to manage, however, and the use of teams can lead to higher employment costs. They make the most sense when service delivery is complex and multiple skill sets are required to provide quality service.[10]

In-house or Outsourced?

This dimension asks the company to choose between owning its service delivery resources and relying on outside sources for them. This dimension applies both to tangible resources and human resources. Variable staffing options, for example, include use of part-time employees, seasonal workers, contracted staff, and even outsourcing overflow to service partners. In a similar manner, facilities and equipment can be owned or rented. One retailer may own all store locations whereas another may choose to rent. One university may choose to have its own employees teach classes, whereas another may contract faculty for only individual classes, as in the model used by the University of Phoenix. From a business model perspective, resource ownership increases fixed costs and restricts short-term flexibility. In contrast, an outsource model leads to higher variable costs but to resources that can be more quickly matched to changing customer needs. A company may also choose to outsource only particular steps in service delivery, relying on an outsourcing partner when the partner has particular skills in an area. This is especially likely if the service delivery step requires specialized skills or assets that are not among the company's core competencies. In such cases, a partnership expands the company's capabilities. Outsourced service delivery, however, increases coordination challenges and makes quality more difficult to control.

High Commitment or Low Commitment?

This dimension deals with the company's commitment to its employees. A high-commitment organization views its employees as assets that are appreciated and developed for their value to the company. A low-commitment organization, in contrast, views its employees as disposable resources. A high-commitment organization is characterized by job security, selectivity in hiring, high total compensation, monetary and nonmonetary incentives, employee ownership, information sharing, broad job responsibilities, promotion and development opportunities, and mutual trust.[11] A high-commitment organization requires a larger financial investment in employees. However, it develops a sustainable source of competitive advantage that contributes to long-term success. Further, costs due to employee turnover and poor quality can be significantly reduced in a high-commitment organization.

Other Design Considerations

The list of service delivery dimensions in Figure 7-1, while comprehensive, does not exhaust all the ways in which a service can be differentiated or positioned against the competition. In particular, these dimensions relate to *how* service is delivered rather than *what* is delivered. To put it another way, they pertain to doing things right rather than doing the right things. As discussed throughout this book, a company can understand *what* things to do by uncovering the struggles that customers have in getting a job done. People, technology, tools, and other offerings are then aligned to address these struggles.

From a marketing perspective, other valuable differentiation and positioning decisions include which customers or segments are targeted, how much emphasis to give to getting functional jobs done and how much to place on getting emotional jobs done, and whether to follow a premium or a basic positioning and pricing approach. On the pricing front, the company also has options in terms of how pricing is structured. Customers can pay for service according to use, or the company may have a fixed payment amount or schedule unrelated to use. Flat-rate pricing is easier for customers to understand, though it is less directly connected to the service benefits. The company should also consider what elements of service delivery a customer will pay for and which will be provided "free" but funded through revenue generated in other ways or via cost savings.[12]

From an operations perspective, the company must also consider when processes are executed. Could service delivery processes take place earlier or later than they do currently? If the timing were changed, would this have a positive impact on customer, employee, or company outcomes? In particular, can some things be prepared in advance, before the customer engages the service system? Can processes that currently take place sequentially be executed in parallel? Can certain processes be executed more or less often, or with longer or shorter duration? Behavioral science also provides some interesting insights into how to design service processes. Scientific studies regarding how people experience time and events reveal that finishing strong is even more important than starting strong, that bad experiences should be gotten out of the way early, that bad experiences should be bundled together, that favorable experiences should be unbundled, that customers appreciate choices (but not too many) regarding how a service is provided, and that customers appreciate familiar rituals for how service is delivered.[13] Finally, as information technology becomes more central to effective service delivery, the company must consider what information it will provide to customers, when it will provide the information, and how it will organize the information.

From a human resources perspective, other valuable considerations include the number of employees to dedicate to different delivery tasks, the length of time employees are assigned to serve a given customer, what type of compensation to use (salaries or incentive compensation), how much emphasis to place on hard employee skills and how much on soft skills, how much emphasis to place on quality and how much on quantity in performance evaluations, and the scope of individual responsibilities. Regarding scope, some companies have effectively differentiated their service by giving some service employees complete responsibility for serving customer needs from end to end, or at least giving them an oversight role to ensure that other service activities are coordinated.

Discover Points of Service Delivery Differentiation

Although a company may find value in simply considering design options for a current or new service without bothering to address the issue of customer outcomes, doing so risks misplaced priorities. Customer job and outcome opportunities should be uncovered and prioritized before design decisions are made to ensure that optimal choices and trade-offs are made. Once these priorities are known, a company can use the combination of the universal job map for providing service (Figure 6-1) and the strategic design options discussed in this chapter to systematically consider how to deliver service that will be unique and valuable.

For the overall service, the company must define a strategy that reflects the trade-offs it is willing to make for each of the service delivery dimensions in order to achieve the optimal alignment between high-opportunity customer, employee, and company outcomes. The company should ask the following questions:

- Looking at the various service delivery dimensions, what are the conventional choices for the service in your company and in the industry as a whole, and how do these choices contribute to customer, employee, and company outcome opportunities?
- What are some unconventional ways of providing service that might satisfy these customer (and company and service employee) needs better? Can some conventional choices be combined with unconventional choices?
- Are the potential trade-offs of taking a new service delivery approach worth it in terms of extra value for the customer or greater revenue generation or cost savings for the company? Can the potential trade-offs be overcome?

Summary

Once customer needs are known, it is time for the company to tackle the challenging task of creating (or improving) a service that provides value to the customer in a manner that is differentiated from the competition. Without a structure to guide the process, the task can be overwhelming. What options are available? What considerations apply to each option? This chapter has introduced 20 strategic dimensions along which services vary. These dimensions reflect the expanded seven P's of the services marketing mix—product, price, place, promotion, processes, physical evidence, and people.

Although not exhaustive, the dimensions of Figure 7-1 are the primary ones by which service delivery is differentiated. Further, these dimensions are strategic because they impact not only customer outcomes but also the outcomes of the company and service providers. In fact, many of these dimensions lead not only to new service delivery models but also to new business models because they directly tie to how revenue is generated and how costs are controlled.

By understanding the primary service delivery options available, a company is better prepared to create service concepts that are meaningfully differentiated from competitive services and to avoid overlooking key options or considerations. In combination with the universal job map for providing service, the design options prepare a company to create detailed concepts that will deliver enhanced value.

CHAPTER 8

DEFINE INNOVATIVE SERVICE CONCEPTS

Service innovation is the process of devising new or improved service concepts that satisfy the customer's unmet needs. Success at service innovation first requires discovering what these unmet needs are. Because so much confusion exists concerning how to accomplish this, the majority of this book has addressed that topic.

But understanding customers' unmet needs is only half the picture. A company must then create innovative service concepts to address these needs. There is less confusion about this half of the picture; the trick is making sure the service concepts the company creates are aligned with customers' needs, and that is where having a disciplined approach to devising new and improved service concepts is invaluable. A disciplined approach helps the company to think through the details of what a service concept is, focuses the company's creativity, and helps the company avoid problems in development and delivery.

This chapter begins with a detailed consideration of how to develop a service strategy and define an innovative service concept. It then introduces a step-by-step process for improving a current service or creating a new one, building on the foundation provided by the earlier chapters.

Develop a Service Strategy

A service strategy defines the position that a company wants to occupy with its services.[1] It should be one that is valuable to customers and well differentiated from competitive offerings. A company's service strategy answers the following questions:

- What are the needs of important market segments? What other characteristics do segment members share? Which segment or segments are most attractive for our company?
- What service elements of unique value will we offer to customers? What does this suggest in terms of service design from a marketing, operations, and human resources perspective? What does this suggest in terms of the features of the service system, such as facility design, equipment, and policies?
- What enabling processes must be in place to support the service concept in terms of marketing, operations, human resources, information systems, finance, organizational structure, and control? Where are investments required?

A critical component of a service strategy is the service concept. A *service concept* is a description of the service and how it satisfies customer needs. The service concept should call attention to the differentiating features of the service and how the service helps customers accomplish the job they are trying to get done and achieve the outcomes they are hoping to satisfy in hiring a service for the job. In other words, the service concept should specify what the service provides to customers to satisfy their needs and how the service delivery system is designed to provide customer and company value. The connection between the service's key features and processes and customer jobs and outcomes should be clear. Figure 8-1 provides a structure that can be used for documenting a service concept.

The service strategy should take into account the perspectives of the customer, the company, and the competition. As discussed throughout this book, the key considerations from a customer perspective are these:

Figure 8-1   Service Concept Worksheet Template

Concept Name:	
A descriptive and memorable name	
Concept Description:	
A high-level description of what the service is in terms of what it does for the customer and what makes it unique and valuable; possibly a description of the target customer	
Concept Features:	**Feature Justifications:**
Key features or offerings that deliver value to the customer	Justification based on specific outcomes, related jobs, or emotional jobs of customers
Key design dimensions that make the service unique and valuable	Justification based on specific outcomes, related jobs, or emotional jobs of customers
Key service system characteristics, such as the role of people, technology, and procedures	Justification based on specific outcomes, related jobs, or emotional jobs of customers
Concept Visual:	
A concept rendering or preliminary service blueprint, including identification of key supporting processes and systems	

- What job is the customer trying to get done? What related jobs are customers struggling to get done? What emotional jobs are customers trying to get done? Among these, which jobs represent the greatest opportunity for the company to offer value?
- What are customers' high-opportunity outcomes in getting the core job done? What are the customers' most important outcomes—including those that are already well satisfied—in getting the core job done? What are customers' least important outcomes in getting the core job done?
- What are customers' high-opportunity outcomes in obtaining service? What are the customers' most important outcomes—including those that are already well satisfied—in obtaining service? What are customers' least important outcomes in obtaining service?

Segmentation

Because not all customers share the same job and outcome priorities, a company can also benefit from answering these questions for distinct customer segments in the market. Market segmentation identifies specific groups of customers who share similar needs, needs that distinct service strategies might satisfy. By choosing a promising market segment, the company can focus its resources on opportunities that are most aligned with its capabilities. The company can focus its service strategy and make sensible trade-off decisions when considering service features and delivery options. As Michael Porter has contended, "In general, value is destroyed if an activity is overdesigned or underdesigned for its use."[2]

A service strategy that aligns with the high-opportunity jobs and outcomes of a specific customer segment provides better value to both the customer and the company. If customers are segmented based on which jobs and/or outcomes they consider important but not well satisfied, then the segmentation process will reveal distinct segments of opportunity.[3] This is optimal for developing a focused service strategy. The company can then choose to create unique service offerings targeting one or more of the segments. A segment should be considered more attractive (1) if it presents opportunities that the company knows it can address based on its strategy, capabilities, resources, and access to the segment and (2) if it is likely to produce favorable financial returns.

When TD Bank, for example, wanted to discover opportunities to help customers with managing day-to-day cash flow, it didn't stop with the prioritization of customer outcomes for the total market. Among the 82 customer outcomes that TD Bank uncovered for customers, it identified 11 that could be used to represent the remaining outcomes (on the basis of factor analysis) and that showed the most variation among customers in the level of opportunity (using a calculation for individual opportunity for each outcome). Using these 11 outcomes as inputs into cluster analysis revealed four segments that would require distinct service strategies. These segments could be distinguished by the degree to which they were proactive in managing cash flow and by their reasons for managing cash flow (some managed their money with the intention of getting ahead, while others were concerned with just getting by). TD Bank then evaluated the attractiveness of the distinct segments and focused its strategy and concept creation efforts on the segments that best aligned with its capabilities and objectives.

Value Creation for the Company and Service Providers

The service strategy must create value both for customers *and* for the company and service providers. As noted services expert Len Berry has concluded, "Identifying a service strategy boils down to searching for a match between what needs to be done and what the firm can do exceedingly well."[4] Value creation for the company depends on its ability to deliver consistent quality in a profitable manner. By investing in getting service right at the critical points in the job of providing service, many breakthrough services are able to deliver better value to the customer and keep costs the same or lower than competitive offerings.[5] From a service provider perspective, the service strategy must not only make it possible for providers to deliver the service, it must also include consideration of how providers will respond in terms of job satisfaction. How are pay, opportunities for advancement, job security, and scope of responsibility affected by the service concept? Similar considerations apply for potential service partners.

The Competition

Finally, the service strategy must consider the strengths and weaknesses of competitive offerings. Strategy is about choosing not only what the company will do well but also what the company will *not* do well relative to the competition when the available solution options necessitate a trade-off. For example, Commerce Bank has chosen to deliver value on the basis of extended hours, friendly employees, and attractive branch environments while choosing not to deliver value on the basis of finance rates or wide product selection—areas in which Commerce Bank's competitors are strong.[6] The best basis for making these choices is the priority among customer needs. A company can look for high-opportunity customer needs that the competition is not addressing well and target them. Such unique positions are especially likely to reveal themselves among the opportunities of distinct customer segments.

Define Innovative Service Concepts

Once you have discovered customers' job and/or outcome opportunities, it's time to think of new services and service features that can speak to their unmet needs. Here, in a departure from common practice, wild scattershot brainstorming is replaced by focused idea generation. Instead of the hundreds of concepts that unfocused brainstorming produces, most of which will be irrelevant and useless, focused idea generation produces a handful of service features or process improvements (when improving a current service) or service concept alternatives (when creating a new service) that, by virtue of the focus on high-opportunity customer jobs and outcomes, are guaranteed to be valuable to customers. Following are four principles to ensure success in this process.

First, focus creative energies on specific job and outcome opportunities. There are a variety of creativity techniques out there, and they are fine as complements to anything I will recommend. However, the best input remains a well-defined customer need statement—either a job statement or an outcome statement. The idea generation team must be continually reminded to stay focused on the high-opportunity jobs and outcomes. Expectations should be established up front, and new service ideas should be justified on the basis of the jobs and outcomes they address. Such focus is immensely valuable. A focus on specific high-opportunity outcomes takes the guesswork out of the process. As Ben Allen, CEO of Kroll and former Kroll Ontrack president, explained, "If you know the outcomes that you are trying to solve, your innovation is focused. You don't spend time and money innovating against any outcome that the customer doesn't care about or is already completely satisfied with."[7]

Before idea generation begins, the company should decide whether it wants to improve a current service or create an entirely new service. When the focus is on additional jobs that the customer would like to accomplish (Chapter 2), the choice will likely be to create a new service, though some related jobs may require only that additional features or offerings be added to a current service. When the focus is upon the struggles the customer has in getting a core job done (Chapter 3) or in obtaining service (Chapter 4), then either improvement of a current service or creation of a new service may be the answer. When possible, it is preferable to redesign a current service rather than create a new one. New services come with greater risk and considerably higher investment. However, this decision depends on whether a current service can be fixed. The following questions are key: Which outcomes, related jobs, and emotional jobs can be addressed by adding features to a current service or changing how service is provided? Which current service? Which customer jobs and outcomes will require a new service or service model?

In choosing specific jobs and/or outcomes for focused idea generation, a company should consider areas of overlap among the high-opportunity needs of customers, providers, and the company. For example, both the financial adviser and the customer may have high-opportunity outcomes related to making sure that all client goals are uncovered and reducing the time it takes to capture all relevant client information. In this case, it is apparent that solving the needs of one group will also satisfy the needs of the other. This makes it an especially fruitful area for service innovation. Sometimes, on the other hand, the different stakeholders' needs may appear conflicting. For example, patients want to ensure that all their questions are answered, but physicians want to minimize the amount of time they spend answering patient questions. However, although these needs appear to conflict, this is only true when one considers a narrow definition of the service process, that is, face-to-face interaction. In fact, there may be many creative solutions that satisfy the outcomes of both the patient and the physician. If both perspectives are considered when generating and evaluating new and improved service ideas, this can lead to some very innovative service offerings.

Second, identify where the key problems lie in satisfying high-opportunity jobs and outcomes. To come up with the best ideas, you must understand what is causing the job or outcome to be a high opportunity today. A key consideration for services is whether there is an objective problem or whether it is just a perceptual issue. Because customers struggle to evaluate the quality of many services—especially those parts of service delivery that take place backstage—it is possible that objective quality is good, but perceptions are poor. For example, patients might report low satisfaction with the outcome *increase the likelihood that the medical provider recommends the optimal treatment plan.* However, the problem may not lie with the treatment plan, which may indeed be the best. The patient simply may not realize how much deliberation, research, and comparison the doctor put into the decision of the treatment plan. In such a case, the best solution might be to provide the customer evidence of service quality and to ensure that the tangible clues of the service create the right perceptions.

When the problem is more than perceptual, the company must understand the contributing factors. For core or related-job opportunities, consider context. How does the context in which the job is executed—the *where, when, how,* and *with whom* of job execution—contribute to the struggles the customer is experiencing? When thinking about possible solutions, consider the limitations of current solutions. What is it about current solutions that prevent them from satisfying customers' needs?

When a current service is the primary solution, this question might be restated: "What are the primary reasons why the service fails to satisfy the customer need today?" Depending on the customer need, it may be useful to consider which steps in the universal job map for providing service (Figure 6-1) contribute most to the opportunity.

To further guide consideration of the primary causes of service failure, Figure 8-2 provides a generic fishbone cause-and-effect diagram that can be used to classify potential reasons for poor customer need satisfaction. With a particular job or outcome opportunity in mind, a team of knowledgeable insiders lists the causes contributing to the opportunity in each area of the diagram. The predefined "bones" in Figure 8-2 ensure that a broad selection of possible causes is considered. From among this sizable number of possible causes, the goal is to identify the few controllable causes that contribute the most to failure to help get the job done or to satisfy the desired outcome. Those are areas that might benefit the most from service innovation.

Third, systematically consider a diverse set of new service ideas to satisfy the opportunities. There are a variety of ways to satisfy any job or outcome, and it is unlikely that the first idea will be the best. In fact, the best idea often combines a number of other ideas for satisfying the need. Idea generation should be structured to consider solutions from multiple different perspectives. One way to do this is by ensuring that your idea generation team is a diverse group of creative people—its members should be those individuals who are always coming up with valuable new ways of doing things and who are willing to challenge convention in order to achieve the intended goal. The team also needs individuals who understand the customer, the context in which the job is executed, and the current service solution (when a current service is being improved). The greater the involvement of the customer in getting the job

Figure 8-2 Service Fishbone Diagram

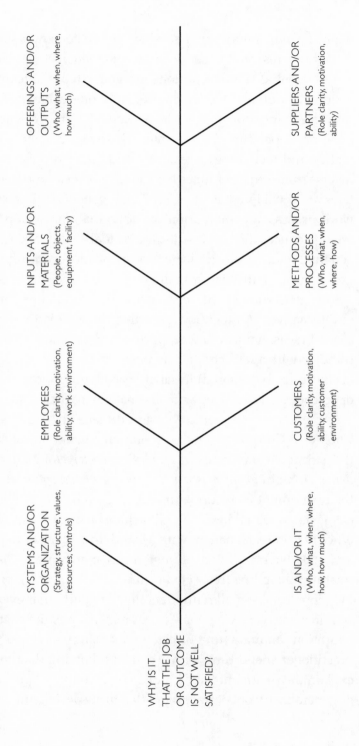

SYSTEMS AND/OR ORGANIZATION
(Strategy, structure, values, resources, controls)

EMPLOYEES
(Role clarity, motivation, ability, work environment)

INPUTS AND/OR MATERIALS
(People, objects, equipment, facility)

OFFERINGS AND/OR OUTPUTS
(Who, what, when, where, how much)

WHY IS IT THAT THE JOB OR OUTCOME IS NOT WELL SATISFIED?

IS AND/OR IT
(Who, what, when, where, how much)

CUSTOMERS
(Role clarity, motivation, ability customer environment)

METHODS AND/OR PROCESSES
(Who, what, when, where, how)

SUPPLIERS AND/OR PARTNERS
(Role clarity, motivation, ability)

done, the more important it is to have the customer perspective directly represented in service concept creation.

As potential solution options are generated, the team will need the perspective of marketing, operations, human resources, and information technology (IT) represented. In addition, depending on the service, there may be other subject matter and technology areas that should be represented. A diverse group ensures that a broad range of ideas and perspectives are considered as ideas are being generated. In terms of work process, a combination of individual and group work often produces the best results. Individuals first work alone to generate alternative service concepts or ideas, and then the group meets to discuss, combine, and refine the concepts.

Idea generation should be structured to force consideration of alternatives. As mentioned earlier, the goal is to generate several ideas, not just one, so participants should be asked to come up with a number of different ways the service might be designed (or redesigned) to satisfy each high-opportunity job or outcome. In coming up with alternatives, participants should consider each of the service design dimensions discussed in Chapter 7. Consider an idea generation session on satisfying the patient outcome *minimize the likelihood of forgetting any actions that are required to implement a recommended treatment plan.* Ideas the team might come up with, focusing on the service design elements discussed in Chapter 7, include having the physician's office provide each patient with a standardized list of required activities (standardized or customized); creating a 24-hour treatment help line (restricted or unrestricted access); providing mobile and e-mail reminders timed to particular events or activities (delivery via people or equipment); hosting customer education seminars (unit or batch processing); having a nurse practitioner spend time with a patient following diagnosis to explain the treatment plan (coupled or decoupled, specialized or generalized); or contracting with a firm specializing in personalized treatment assistance to support patient needs for certain diseases (in-house or outsourced, standardized or customized, equal or unequal treatment, bundled or unbundled offerings, delivery via people or equipment, and so on).

In addition, the following questions are especially helpful for stimulating the generation of a diverse set of innovative ideas:

- *How have those in other industries dealt with similar customer or service delivery struggles?* One of the benefits of the universal job maps is that they facilitate comparisons across industries, including nonservice industries. For example, the Nike+ iPod Sport Kit allows runners to track their progress against predefined goals by synchronizing workout data with nikeplus.com. Might a bank enable its customers to track spending against predefined goals in much the same way?
- *What are some examples of solutions or workarounds that customers have created to satisfy the high-opportunity jobs or outcomes?* For example, some customers save money by having the government withhold more from their paychecks than necessary. A bank could set up an automatic savings plan that deducts a certain amount of money from automatic paycheck deposits and keeps it in a separate restricted account.
- *What is a far-fetched idea for perfect completion of the job or attainment of the outcomes?* For example, it may be far-fetched to expect a personal nutrition expert to be with a dieter for every meal. However, this can be made practical by creating a mobile application that is always with the dieter to answer key nutrition questions.

Fourth, build a detailed concept with service strategy and service delivery in mind. There are two stages to creating new service concepts. First, there is the process of developing a high-level concept that provides a general description of the proposed new service and how it creates value for customers relative to the competition. Given the various considerations in developing a service strategy, each high-level service concept should be evaluated and refined with several questions in mind:

- Does the service concept satisfy customer needs in a unique and meaningful way? Will the service concept deliver meaningful value to a customer segment at a sustainable price?
- Does the service concept make the appropriate trade-offs between benefits and costs and among different constituencies—customers, company, providers, partners, and so on? How will service providers respond to the concept?
- Are the service concept features and design elements internally consistent? Is there synergy among them? Is it clear how quality and costs will be controlled?
- Can the company develop and deliver on the service concept as designed? What new capabilities or resources will be required? Is the time it will take to develop the service justified by the value created? Are the costs of developing the service justified by the value created?

Once the service concept gets the go-ahead, additional detail should be added to the concept to guide development. The detailed concept design must anticipate what it will take to successfully deliver on the new or improved service. For a new service, in particular, it is important to consider the entire job-to-be-done from a customer and provider perspective. What must happen at each step to ensure success in getting the job done? For detailing how a new or improved service should be delivered, a service blueprint should be created. "Blueprints are particularly useful at the design stage of service development. A service blueprint visually displays the service by simultaneously depicting the process of service delivery, the points of customer contact, the roles of customers and providers, and the visible elements of the service."[8] A service blueprint helps the company to develop the service concept by making clear (1) the sequence of service activities for distinct customer segments, (2) what takes place in the presence and absence of the customer, (3) required handoffs among providers, (4) potential fail points in service delivery, and (5) physical evidence and support requirements.[9] Figure 8-3 combines Chapter 4's job map for obtaining service with Chapter 6's job map for providing service. The resultant job map of service delivery can be used to guide the blueprinting of a specific service (see also the questions at the close of Chapter 6).

To ensure success, a detailed service concept design must anticipate what it will take to actually deliver the service. Critical to service delivery are the following:

- Facility design
- Technology (materials, methods, and information management systems)
- Equipment
- Processes, policies, and controls (including service standards)
- The employee management system (job design, selection, training, evaluation, feedback and control, and compensation and incentive systems)
- The customer management system (possibly job design, selection, training, evaluation, feedback and control, and reward systems)
- Service partners and suppliers (possibly job design, selection, training, evaluation, feedback and control, and reward systems)
- Deliverables, supplies, and tangible evidence [10]

Figure 8-3   Universal Service Delivery Job Map

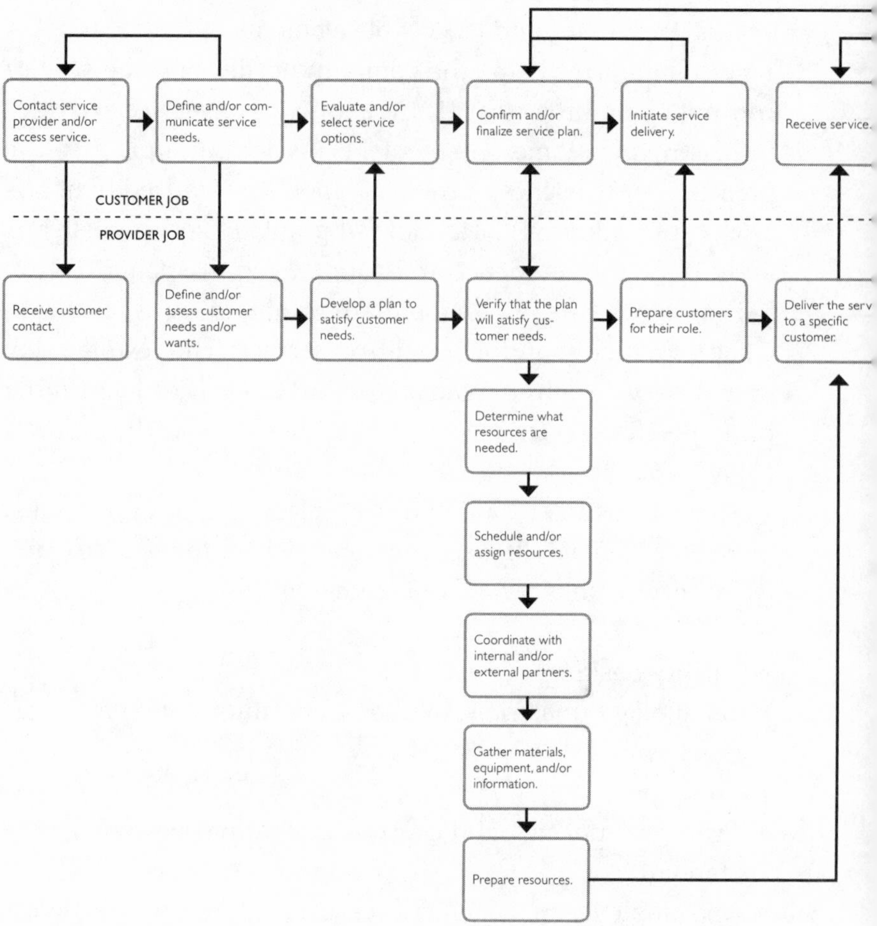

For each area, a company should answer the following questions: What new capabilities or resources will be required to deliver the service? What must be developed or modified to deliver the service? What actions must be taken? With regard to providers, customers, and service partners specifically, the company must consider what it will take to ensure that each

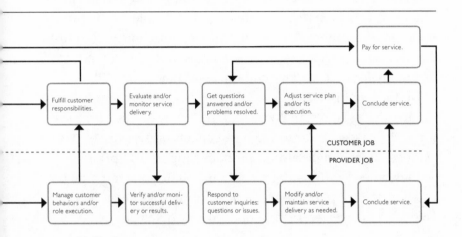

group knows what its role entails and is able and motivated to perform this role in an exceptional manner. Specific actions in each area can then be assigned a timetable and given to specific individuals or teams for development.

Improve a Current Service

When the goal is to improve a current service, your inputs are typically customer outcomes for a core job or the consumption chain job of obtaining service. The simplest approach, and often the preferred approach, is to generate service improvement ideas for the highest-opportunity outcomes (for the total sample or by segment) one at a time. Of course, if there are overlapping high-opportunity outcomes from the customer and provider perspective, it may be very useful to place these together. This is especially true if satisfying the outcomes for one perspective has traditionally come at the expense of the other. Very closely related outcomes of customers may also be considered together, especially if there is reason to believe that a common solution is necessary or possible. If there are different service delivery approaches (for example, self-service, personal service) or service products (for example, credit card, savings account) or if different segments or contexts require distinct service processes, then ideas should be considered separately for each variation of interest to the company.

We followed this process with a medical equipment manufacturer, for example, that was seeking to improve its technical support services. Prior to the idea generation session, we had mapped the job of obtaining product support and prioritized the outcomes by surveying more than 250 surgical nurses who relied on the support of our client or one of its key competitors. This process revealed 15 high-opportunity outcomes that could be divided into 10 groups for idea generation. The outcome opportunities spanned a number of steps on the job map for obtaining product support (Figure 5-1), including contacting support (for example, *minimize the number of times the company must be contacted to get a problem resolved*), getting a support response (for example, *minimize the time it takes to get a service person to the facility once technical support has been arranged*), and explaining the support problem (for example, *minimize the number of times the same information must be provided to the company to get a problem resolved*).

Once the outcome opportunities were identified, employees representing sales, marketing, field service, and support worked together to identify the key reasons why current service was not satisfying the outcomes. Relying on the universal job map for providing service (Figure 6-1), they identified which steps were the biggest contributors to a particular outcome opportunity. To maintain the scope, the team decided to focus on as few steps as possible for any given outcome opportunity. For example, the team determined that support response time was limited in particular by problems during (1) scheduling or assigning resources and (2) coordinating with internal partners. For each outcome opportunity, company insiders relied on the fishbone diagram in Figure 8-2 to facilitate a discussion of the key causes of ineffective service.[11] As described earlier, they discussed these causes separately for the key service provision steps and for the outcome itself. During the discussion, they used the service design dimensions outlined in Chapter 7 (Figures 7-1 and 7-2) to aid in the diagnosis.

This process revealed a large number of problem areas. For the outcome *minimize the time it takes to get a service person to the facility once technical support has been arranged*, for example, company insiders identified multiple problems, including the following:

- Field service dispatch prioritization is inadequate, stemming from poor diagnosis.
- Technical support does not know the status of field service availability.
- Field service does not have the same information that technical support has.

The team chose to focus idea generation on the handful of problems (three to five) that had the biggest impact, were controllable by the company, and were likely to be addressable with solutions the company could implement.

The group then turned to generating service improvement ideas to satisfy each of the top problems identified for a given outcome. For each problem, teams generated service feature and/or process improvements. To guide the idea generation process, they considered the design dimensions of Figure 7-1 and also best practices that had been gathered beforehand. After removing redundant ideas, the team looked for logical combinations of ideas that were generated for different problems (even if the problems were tied to distinct outcomes). For example, the team came up with multiple service improvement ideas for improving data capture and availability that could be handled through an improved information management system. These included ideas related to using information technology to diagnose the urgency of the technical support problem, determine the availability of field service staff, dispatch field service, and stay up-to-date on field service progress.

In the above example, it made sense to combine ideas, but the team should resist the temptation to place *all* ideas into logical groups at this point. Ideas should not be combined unless the evaluation process will be enhanced by having them combined, and this must be determined on a case-by-case basis. In many cases, individual improvement features should be kept separate because they do not depend on other ideas for their value. This is especially true when the ideas have different time horizons for their likely implementation.[12]

The team prioritized the ideas they had generated by considering which would best satisfy the outcome opportunities in the most cost-effective manner, how much time implementation would take, and how great the risk was that the company would not be able to deliver on the improvement idea based on company capabilities, strategy alignment, and other boundaries of the idea generation process. It then created detailed designs for approved ideas, taking into account facility, technology, equipment, process, employee management, customer management, partners and/or suppliers, and deliverable development requirements. For example, an idea for remote equipment monitoring included the following design details:

- *Facilities.* Customer sites will need to be prepared for connectivity.
- *Equipment.* We will need a dedicated server, hardware and software hooks, and network connection on equipment.
- *Procedures.* We will need to develop a technical support process to act on received information.

- *Suppliers.* We will need to provide a requirements road map for equipment suppliers.
- *Deliverables.* The data format will need to be worked out to provide insight to the equipment operator and technical support.

Create a New Service

When the goal is to create a new service or redesign a current service from the ground up, you may be working with jobs, outcomes on a core job, or outcomes on obtaining service (and possibly providing service). When working with customer job opportunities, the company must first decide which jobs to pursue with service innovation. As described in Chapter 1, this decision relies on prioritization of different jobs using criteria much like those used to prioritize a product portfolio. Customer jobs are prioritized for service innovation based on considerations of revenue potential, level of opportunity, alignment with strategy, ability to create and sustain a leadership position, and any social or financial risks from pursuing them. Before creating a new service for a job opportunity, a company should capture outcomes on the job using the universal job map from Chapter 3. However, at times, a high-opportunity job may be revealed for which there are no good solutions out there today—service or otherwise. In this case, it is possible (though still not preferable) to create a very valuable new service without having a detailed set of customer outcomes. The universal job map of a core job (Figure 3-1) can still be your guide to creating the new service, but only in its universal form.

Whether working with a single high-opportunity job, outcome opportunities on a core job, or outcome opportunities on obtaining service, the key question that will guide new service creation is this: where do customers struggle the most in getting the job done? If the outcome opportunities vary meaning-fully from customer segment to segment, then the company may want to consider the top 15 to 20 outcome opportunities and a handful of emotional job opportunities for the customer segment that is most attractive to it. With these opportunities in mind, it will be useful to consider any apparent value themes to guide the process of setting objectives for the new service. For example, a company may find a segment of pregnant women with high opportunities pertaining to getting optimal nutrition for self and baby, getting insight into the body's response to nutrition intake, and having nutritious food available when on the go. These themes derive from two or more outcome opportunities that span steps in the core job of getting the right nutrients while pregnant. As for emotional jobs, these same women want to *feel in control, feel reassured,* and *avoid feeling stressed.*

There are two complementary approaches that a company can take to structuring idea generation for new service concepts. First, it can identify the most important steps in the core customer job and use these to guide the generation of new service concepts. Second, it can identify the most important steps in the job map for providing service and use them to guide the generation of new service concepts.[13] In either case, the steps that are most important are those which have a large impact on the customer opportunities and offer the best potential for competitive service differentiation.[14]

To continue with the example of the pregnant women who are concerned about prenatal nutrition, there are a handful of important steps in the core job related to the outcome opportunities, including planning what to eat, selecting specific food and/or beverage items, consuming foods, providing an optimal environment for the baby, and assessing and adjusting one's diet. From the perspective of the job of providing service, key steps might include defining and/or assessing customer needs, developing a plan to satisfy customer needs, preparing customers for their role, delivering the service, and verifying and/or monitoring successful delivery or results.

For each of the key steps from one or both of these approaches, the company should develop a service design objective that specifies what the new service must accomplish to satisfy customer and company needs. The objective is stated from the service perspective, but with customer needs playing a starring role. In addition to outcome and emotional job opportunities, other important but well-satisfied customer outcomes may also be considered in order to avoid undesirable trade-offs. In addition, desired service positioning and key problems that customers experience with current solutions may be considered. For the core job steps in our example, the objectives might be the following:

- *Plan what to eat.* To understand expectant women's specific nutrient needs and also their diet, lifestyle, and health priorities so an optimal plan can be developed for them.
- *Select specific food and beverage items.* To help expectant women make intelligent and confident food choices to fulfill the plan with no unexpected physical side effects.
- *Consume foods.* To provide expectant women with nutritious food choices that they want to eat—when and where they need them—to ensure that they stay on track with healthy eating.
- *Provide an optimal environment for the baby.* To ensure that expectant women get all the nutrients their bodies need to support their daily activities and reassure them that they are doing all they can to give their babies a head start in life.

- *Assess and adjust one's diet.* To provide expectant women with the insight they require to know how they are doing and to make adjustments in their diet based on how they feel, and to reassure them that they are making the right choices and doing their best.

With these objectives, it's time for a team of company insiders to be creative. Because in this case the task is to develop a new service, the team does not require specific insight into how current service processes work, but it does need to have a good understanding of the customer, company strategy, and market environment. For each important step that has been identified, the team works individually and as a group to identify different service delivery approaches and offerings to fulfill the service design objective for that step.[15] The key question to be answered by the ideas generated is this: what are the different ways in which the service design objective might be satisfied? Whereas the focus for improving a current service can be service delivery *or* backstage support processes, the focus for new service creation is squarely on alternative service delivery approaches and offerings. Once again, however, the team should review the design dimensions in Chapter 7 to stimulate creative service delivery ideas. The columns labeled "Job Steps" and "Alternative Service Approaches or Offerings" in Figure 8-4 provide a hypothetical sampling of ideas by job step for our prenatal nutrition example.

Once various ideas have been generated for each job step, the team begins to formulate high-level service concepts by combining ideas from across the different steps in unique, meaningful, and synergistic ways. Of course, redundant ideas and obviously infeasible ideas can be eliminated at this point. These initial concepts can be further refined based on ideas from alternative concepts or even ideas that were left on the table. Following a discussion to ensure a common understanding of the concept, and following consideration of what the complete service will look like given other steps in the job map, the team then adds additional details to each concept. The column labeled "Alternative Service Concept Ideas" in Figure 8-4 provides a summary description of three concept ideas that resulted from this process for our prenatal nutrition example.

Finally, the team must select and refine the best service concept. Concept evaluation relies on comparisons among individual concepts based on a set of criteria that includes customer needs (for example, top opportunities plus other important outcomes as well as cost and adoption likelihood); service provider needs (for example, provider opportunities, likely concept acceptance); and company needs (for example, financial objectives, strategy alignment, sustainability, time and cost to develop, technical risk, service concept boundaries). The team weights the evaluation criteria, rates the individual concepts against each criterion, and then sums the weights multiplied by concept ratings to distinguish better from worse concepts. The team then explores design modifications to eliminate any weaknesses and to strengthen the strengths in the best concept. These improvement ideas can come from anywhere, including the other concepts. The concept comparison and refinement process may be repeated if this process generates competing alternatives. The final service concept is summarized using a worksheet such as Figure 8-1, and a detailed service design is developed as described earlier in the chapter. With an innovative service concept in hand, it's now time for service development to take over.[16]

Figure 8-4   New Service Innovation Illustration

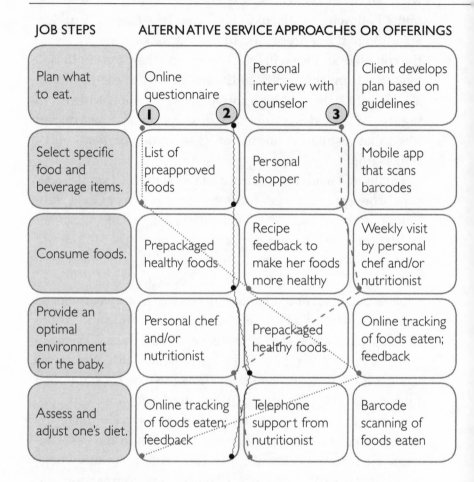

JOB STEPS	ALTERNATIVE SERVICE APPROACHES OR OFFERINGS		
Plan what to eat.	Online questionnaire ①	Personal interview with counselor	Client develops plan based on guidelines
Select specific food and beverage items.	List of preapproved foods	Personal shopper	Mobile app that scans barcodes
Consume foods.	Prepackaged healthy foods	Recipe feedback to make her foods more healthy	Weekly visit by personal chef and/or nutritionist
Provide an optimal environment for the baby.	Personal chef and/or nutritionist	Prepackaged healthy foods	Online tracking of foods eaten; feedback
Assess and adjust one's diet.	Online tracking of foods eaten; feedback	Telephone support from nutritionist	Barcode scanning of foods eaten

Summary

The best guide to creating a unique and valuable service strategy is a detailed understanding of customer needs—complemented by a systematic process for defining service strategy and innovative service concepts. This chapter has outlined such a process and brought together many complementary insights into service innovation from the rest of the book.

for Prenatal Nutrition

ALTERNATIVE SERVICE CONCEPT IDEAS

 Prenatal do-it-yourselfer

A combination of online tools and assessments based on expert prenatal nutrition guidance that makes recommendations to the client, but allows her the choice of foods based on personal lifestyle, food preferences, and health situation.

 Jenny Craig Prenatal

A selection of preprepared foods for both meals and snacks that is provided to the client based on a wide variety of options that can be tailored to her lifestyle, food preferences, and health situation. A learning system that adapts based on feedback from her.

 The Personal Touch

A dedicated client representative assesses client needs and tailors a diet plan. Client initially receives personal nutrition coaching to make the right nutrition choices, including help with food selection to fulfill the diet plan. Meals and snacks are prepared at the client home on a regular basis. 24/7 phone access to personal health coach.

A service strategy defines the position that a company wants to occupy with its service. It should be one that is valuable to customers and well differentiated from competitive offerings. An effective service strategy reflects the overlap of customer needs (job and outcome opportunities) and company capabilities. It also reflects the position that will most effectively differentiate the service from the competition. A critical component of a service strategy is the service concept, which describes what the service is and how it satisfies customer needs. To define an innovative service concept, a company should accomplish the following:

- Focus creative energies on specific job and outcome opportunities.
- Identify where the key problems lie in satisfying high-opportunity jobs and outcomes.
- Systematically consider a diverse set of new service ideas to satisfy the opportunities.
- Build a detailed concept with service strategy and service delivery in mind.

The process for improving a current service includes understanding the problems that underlie specific high-opportunity outcomes before generating feature and process improvements. The process for creating a new service follows a similar pattern, but it is less concerned with developing specific features to satisfy specific outcomes. Rather, the focus is on generating alternative service delivery approaches for the most important steps in a customer or provider job, considering the range of unmet customer needs (outcomes, emotional jobs, and possibly related jobs). Alternative delivery approaches are then combined and refined to define cohesive service concepts that support a unique and valuable service strategy. Using the approach to defining innovative service concepts outlined in this chapter, companies have the final ingredient they need to make service innovation a systematic and repeatable process.

CONCLUSION
BEYOND *SERVICES* INNOVATION

I have a particular passion for services. I work in a service business. My training at Arizona State University was in services marketing and management. My academic research focused on services. I find the challenges of services compelling. Yet, when I contemplated the literature, I realized that there wasn't much being written about service innovation. I knew we required more insight into the topic. So I set out to write this book.

As I described in the Introduction, my focus has been on the innovation of essentially intangible services, whether by a service- or product-dominant company. Several of the models that I have described have a special relevance for the innovation of services, including the universal job map for obtaining service (Chapter 4), the universal job map for providing service (Chapter 6), the design dimensions by which service delivery is differentiated (Chapter 7), and even much of the content describing how innovative service concepts are created (Chapter 8). In all cases, I strove to make clear how the approach and tools I presented apply to service innovation.

Yet, I would be remiss if I didn't help you to step back and appreciate the relevance of the model I have described for innovation more broadly. The four fundamental truths I discussed in Chapter 1, for example, are as applicable to goods as they are to services:

1. Customers hire products and services to get a job done.
2. Customers hire solutions to accomplish distinct steps in getting an entire job done.
3. Customers use outcomes to evaluate success in getting a job done.
4. Customers have distinct needs that arise related to the "consumption" of a solution.

I have placed these four fundamental truths at the foundation of the search for opportunities for service innovation. Yet, because they are equally applicable to goods, they can also provide the foundation for discovering opportunities for goods or product innovation. Like the innovation of services, product innovation can help customers get a specific job done better or help them get more jobs done. Once a product solution is defined, a company can also innovate by helping customers to "consume" the product. This means that the general guidance provided in Chapter 2 (discovering job opportunities), Chapter 3 (discovering outcome opportunities for a core job), and Chapter 5 (discovering consumption chain opportunities related to a product) can also be applied to product innovation. In fact, if a company is open to either product or service innovation, it can let the opportunities that are discovered inform which type of innovation it should pursue. Some opportunities can be better satisfied through product innovation, and other opportunities can be better satisfied through service innovation. And some require both.

Similarly, there has been a fundamental shift in the past decade within marketing academia, a shift from a goods-dominant logic to a service-dominant logic of marketing.[1] In fact, it is possible that some of you thought this new logic was the focus for this book. My apologies if you did. Still, there is an association between what I have said and this perspective.

A fundamental premise of service-dominant logic is that *service* is what is always exchanged. In other words, both tangible goods and intangible services are hired for the service they render. A digital recorder, for example, offers a recording service to the owner. The goal of service-dominant logic is to shift the focus from the means by which value is delivered and, in so doing, to break down artificial barriers between goods and services marketing, domestic and international marketing, and consumer and business-to-business marketing so that common theory and tools can be applied to all. This should sound familiar if you recall my comments in the Introduction to this book. As explained by proponents of this logic:

> Customers do not buy goods or services: they buy offerings which render services which create value. . . . The traditional division between goods and services is long outdated. It is not a matter of redefining services and seeing them from a customer perspective; activities render services, things render services. The shift in focus to services is a shift from the means and the producer perspective to the utilization and the customer perspective.[2]

In fact, however, though service-dominant logic has laid the foundation for a unifying logic to understand *what* is always exchanged—service—regardless of solution form, customer type, or geographic location, it has not provided a unifying logic for *why* customers exchange. The definitions of customer needs, satisfaction, and value in academic articles and texts seem inevitably to link these terms to the *means* by which value is delivered. Customer needs are described in terms of product requirements and service quality expectations. Customer satisfaction is defined in terms of perceived product or service performance. Customer value is defined in terms of product value, services value, personnel value, and image value.

Unfortunately, as long as the definitions of customer needs, satisfaction, and value are linked to solutions, then approaches to innovation will be as well. When academics or managers confuse solutions, requirements, and quality expectations with customer needs, it is easy to understand why they conclude that service and product innovation require different models. A focus on the solution rather than the customers' needs explains why there are currently efforts under way to develop the science of services innovation, despite the concurrent shift toward a service-dominant logic. As described by Jim Spohrer, a director of service research at IBM, the impetus for the founding of the nonprofit Service Research & Innovation Institute is that "people have a good idea of what technological innovation is. But service innovation is more hidden."[3] On the one hand, I applaud the efforts of this consortium. However, I am concerned that undue focus on services will result in models that apply only to services. And this would be unfortunate.

This leads me to the association between the innovation approach described in this book and service-dominant logic. Customer jobs and outcomes offer the basis for understanding customer needs, satisfaction, and value in a manner that is not tied to any particular solution form, customer type, or geographic location. As such, jobs and outcomes provide the unifying logic for *why* customers exchange. Customer jobs and outcomes are not defined or captured with a particular solution type in mind. In fact, they exist whether a marketplace solution does or not. Further, both consumers and business customers have jobs for which they hire solutions. And customers doing the same job in any part of the world rely on the same outcomes to evaluate success (though they may prioritize them differently). In other words, jobs and outcomes provide the unifying focal point for a service-dominant logic of innovation.[4]

Thus, although I have placed a special focus on the innovation of services in this book due to my passion for the area and my desire to clear up the confusion surrounding it, the basic approach I have advocated really does align with the service-dominant logic of marketing. Are there differences between goods and services? Sure. However, I have been careful to focus only on differences where absolutely necessary. In all other instances, although the context of the discussion is service innovation, the truths discussed apply equally well to product innovation. This is quite intentional. My goal is not to offer a distinct model for service innovation but rather, to show how an effective and efficient model for innovation applies both to products and services. I believe that this book has something very real—something universal—to say about service innovation, however it is defined.

NOTES

Introduction

1. In this book, *service* or *services* refer to those benefits, activities, or processes that are offered by an individual or company to another "that are essentially intangible and do not result in the ownership of anything" (Philip Kotler and Gary Armstrong, *Principles of Marketing* [Upper Saddle River, NJ: Prentice-Hall, 1999], 6).
2. U.S. Census Bureau, 2007 Economic Census. Available at factfinder.census.gov/servlet/IBQTable?_bm=y&-geo_ id=&-ds_name=EC0700CADV1&-_lang=en.
3. Henry Chesbrough, "Toward a New Science of Services," *Harvard Business Review* 83, no. 2 (February 2005), 43–44.
4. Reena Jana, "Service Innovation: The Next Big Thing," *BusinessWeek,* March 29, 2007. Available at www. businessweek.com/innovate/content/mar2007/ id20070329_376916.htm.
5. Robert G. Cooper and Scott J. Edgett, *Product Development for the Service Sector* (New York: Basic Books, 1999), 8.
6. There is a similar confusion between service innovation and service design. For example, while service blueprinting

is an exceptional technique for the design and improvement of a current service, it is not optimal for the creation of new services because one must have a service in mind to begin the blueprinting process.

7. Cooper and Edgett, *Product Development for the Service Sector*, 72.

8. Stefan Thomke, "R&D Comes to Services: Bank of America's Pathbreaking Experiments," *Harvard Business Review* 81, no. 4 (April 2003), 70–79.

9. Cooper and Edgett, *Product Development for the Service Sector*, 60–64.

10. For a good overview of the philosophy and practice of outcome-driven innovation, see Anthony W. Ulwick, *What Customers Want* (New York: McGraw-Hill, 2005).

11. See Lance A. Bettencourt, "Debunking Myths About Customer Needs," *Marketing Management* (January–February 2009), 46–52.

12. Personal communication, February 25, 2009.

Chapter 1

1. Anthony W. Ulwick and Lance A. Bettencourt, "Giving Customers a Fair Hearing," *MIT Sloan Management Review* (Spring 2008): 62–68.

2. Lance A. Bettencourt, "Debunking Myths About Customer Needs," *Marketing Management* (January–February 2009): 46–52.

3. This section only applies to *functional* jobs. Emotional jobs— introduced in Chapter 2—follow a different structure.

4. For additional insight into how customer needs are prioritized and how segments of opportunity can be identified, see Anthony W. Ulwick, *What Customers Want* (New York: McGraw-Hill, 2005).

5. Anthony W. Ulwick, "Turn Customer Input into Innovation," *Harvard Business Review* 80, no. 1 (January 2002): 91–97.

6. Whereas jobs and outcomes with opportunity scores of 10 or higher are considered underserved, we define overserved jobs and outcomes as those for which the satisfaction rating is higher than the importance rating. Overserved needs offer the company the possibility of defeaturing a solution to reduce costs.

7. For an excellent discussion of the elements of a strategic service vision, see James L. Heskett, "Lessons in the Service Sector," *Harvard Business Review* 65, no. 2 (March–April 1987): 118–126.

Chapter 2

1. An interesting variation of this approach is to consider the jobs that customers are trying to get done when using a specific product, since many services help customers accomplish jobs that relate to the job for which they are using a product. For example, the OnStar car security system supports many other jobs that drivers want to get done when using a car, such as contacting emergency services, obtaining roadside assistance, and determining which route to take.

2. A company may restrict the customer to a current target market (for example, high-income customers). However, this should be done only if the company would not serve the excluded customers even if they could be shown to have many high-opportunity jobs of interest to the company. A preferred approach is to define the customer group as broadly as possible and let the job priorities of different customers point to a target market for new services.

3. Many services, in fact, focus on care for something (for example, care for a pet, a lawn, a building, a child, personal health), and this can be a productive area of inquiry.
4. Many services are experienced, but that is not the focus here. Rather, the focus here is uncovering the experience jobs for which a service is or might be hired. This puts it in the realm of innovation rather than design, which focuses on helping the customer have a good service experience.
5. For more on the relationship between services and experiences, see B. Joseph Pine II and James H. Gilmore, *The Experience Economy* (Boston: Harvard Business School Press, 1999).
6. For example, when using a bank, consumers want to feel respected, feel valued, and feel supported.

Chapter 3

1. Some services help or partner with the customer get a job done. For example, Weight Watchers helps customers lose weight, but it doesn't actually lose the weight for them. Other services take over the responsibility for the job from the customer, as with repairing a car. The latter type of service will especially benefit from the core job's being defined in a more abstract manner, as described at the close of this chapter. In addition, these services will benefit from mapping the consumption chain job of obtaining service as discussed in Chapter 4.
2. Lance A. Bettencourt and Anthony W. Ulwick, "The Customer-Centered Innovation Map," *Harvard Business Review* 86, no. 5 (May 2008): 109–114.
3. A *correlation* reveals the strength of the relationship between two variables.

Chapter 4

1. The job of obtaining service for a particular service should also be defined in a manner that transcends the steps of the universal job map once these steps are understood. It would be more insightful for a bank to study the job of obtaining a commercial loan, for example, than applying for a commercial loan, which is one step in obtaining the loan.

2. The steps in the universal job map apply to both new and repeat customers though some steps may be not be repeated each time a service is hired if the customer has a "membership" relationship with the service provider. The job map is, however, primarily applicable to services in which the customer and the service provider interact—whether in person or remotely.

3. Mary Jo Bitner, Amy L. Ostrom, and Felicia N. Morgan, "Service Blueprinting: A Practical Technique for Service Innovation," *California Management Review* 50, no. 3 (Spring 2008): 66–94.

4. Personal communication, September 2, 2009.

5. Though not the focus of this chapter, specific high-opportunity outcomes also led to the acquisition and further innovation of Suppleye.com by AMO. Suppleye.com is a Web-based replenishment system that integrates universal barcode scanning, an online stockroom, and sophisticated online ordering software to enable automatic inventory adjustments and simplified preparation of a lens order based on the completed cases of a surgical center.

Chapter 5

1. This chapter focuses on opportunities a company has to introduce service innovations in support of its own products. That is, it addresses service innovation for companies whose primary focus is their products. Companies that develop service innovations more generally to support products out in the marketplace are not engaged in supplementary service innovation because service innovation is their primary, not their supplementary, focus.
2. See Stephen W. Brown, Anders Gustafsson, and Lars Witell, "Beyond Products," *Wall Street Journal,* June 22, 2009. Available online at online.wsj.com/article/SB10001424052970 2048303045741312731 23644620.html.
3. Personal communication, August 5, 2009.
4. Ian C. MacMillan and Rita Gunther McGrath, "Discovering New Points of Differentiation," *Harvard Business Review* 75 no. 4 (July–August 1997), 133–145.
5. A compressed-air system is used to power various types of industrial machinery.
6. Adrian Slywotzky, Richard Wise, and Karl Weber, *How to Grow When Markets Don't* (New York: Warner Business Books, 2003), 153–169.
7. Personal communication, August 14, 2009.

Chapter 6

1. Valarie Zeithaml, Mary Jo Bitner, and Dwayne Gremler, *Services Marketing: Integrating Customer Focus Across the Firm,* 5th ed. (New York: McGraw-Hill, 2009), 351–355.

2. As always, the job statement will begin with a verb, followed by a specific object of action, but now stated from an internal perspective of what is being done on behalf of the customer. Illustrative job statements for service providers include *resolve a claim, teach a class, serve a meal, sell a car,* and *open an account.*

3. As an interesting exercise, now consider the job of providing a cash withdrawal when a person provides the service. Note that the job map steps are the same.

4. The job map for providing service can be used both to map the job from the perspective of the company as a whole or from the perspective of the actual individuals responsible for providing service. As such, the term *service provider* is used generically throughout the discussion of the job map to refer to either perspective.

5. For more on these techniques, see Christopher Lovelock, *Product Plus* (New York: McGraw-Hill, 1994).

6. Sunil Chopra and Martin A. Lariviere, "Managing Service Inventory to Improve Performance," *MIT Sloan Management Review* 47, no. 1 (Fall 2005): 56–63.

7. See Andrew McAfee and Erik Brynjolfsson, "Dog Eat Dog," *Wall Street Journal*, April 28, 2007, available online at online. wsj.com/article/SB117735476945179344-search.html; and Rob Eder and Antoinette Alexander, "Chains Put Pharmacy First in Strategic Initiatives," *Drug Store News*, August 18, 2003, available online at findarticles.com/p/articles/mi_m3374/is_10_25/ai_108969618/.

8. Jim Cory, "Bird's-Eye View," *Replacement Contractor Magazine*, May 14, 2009. Available online at www. replacementcontractoronline.com/industry-news-print.asp? sectionID=0&articleID=958433.

9. Qm Group, *HSBC Improves Branch Customer Service with Qm's Matchmaker Service* (Milton Keynes, United Kingdom: Qm Group, 2007). Available online at www.cisco.com/web/strategy/docs/finance/HSBC_case_study.pdf.

10. Leonard L. Berry and Kent D. Seltman, "Building a Strong Services Brand: Lessons from Mayo Clinic," *Business Horizons* 50, no. 3 (March 2007): 199–209.

11. John Ouren, "Marketers and Researchers Must Do More to Ensure Real Respondents," CustomerThink.com, February 6, 2009, www.customerthink.com/article/researchers_must_ensure_real_respondents.

12. Lance A. Bettencourt, Amy L. Ostrom, Stephen W. Brown, and Robert I. Roundtree, "Client Co-Production in Knowledge-Intensive Business Services," *California Management Review* 44, no. 4 (Summer 2002): 100–128.

13. Peter Honebein, *Strategies for Effective Customer Education* (Chicago: American Marketing Association, 1997), 120–122.

14. Stephen S. Tax, Mark Colgate, and David E. Bowen, "How to Prevent Your Customers from Failing," *MIT Sloan Management Review* 47, no. 4 (Spring 2006): 30–38.

15. Ritz-Carlton Hotel Company, "Gold Standards," corporate. ritzcarlton.com/en/About/GoldStandards.htm.

16. Each separate job executor group and job overseer group rates a separate set of outcomes for importance and satisfaction. Each group must rate only those outcomes of relevance to their role.

17. Some of these questions are variations of those used in service blueprinting. See, for example, Lovelock, *Product Plus*, 154.

Chapter 7

1. This chapter draws extensively on the rich literature on services marketing, management, and operations. Although the list of service design dimensions presented in this chapter is my own, I have benefited from and relied heavily on this literature. In particular, I am indebted to Jean Harvey, *Managing Service Delivery Processes* (Milwaukee: ASQ Quality Press, 2006); James L. Heskett, W. Earl Sasser, Jr., and Christopher W. L. Hart, *Service Breakthroughs* (New York: Free Press, 1990); Christopher Lovelock, *Product Plus* (New York: McGraw-Hill, 1994); and Valarie Zeithaml, Mary Jo Bitner, and Dwayne Gremler, *Services Marketing: Integrating Customer Focus Across the Firm*, 5th ed. (New York: McGraw-Hill, 2009).

2. Bernard H. Booms and Mary Jo Bitner, "Marketing Strategies and Organizational Structures for Service Firms," in *Marketing of Services*, edited by J. H. Donnelly and W. R. George (Chicago: American Marketing Association, 1981), 47–51.

3. Perhaps noticeably absent from Figure 7-1 is promotion. While very important, promotion is about creating awareness, interest, desire, and action among customers rather than providing a means of satisfying their needs, and therefore it is not relevant to this discussion.

4. Lovelock, *Product Plus*, 49.

5. See Chapter 8's discussion of opportunity segmentation.

6. For an interesting discussion of how to deal with customer-introduced variability, see Frances X. Frei, "Breaking the Trade-off Between Efficiency and Service," *Harvard Business Review* 84, no. 11 (November 2006): 92–101.

7. Leonard L. Berry and Neeli Bendapudi, "Clueing in Customers," *Harvard Business Review* 81, no. 2 (February 2003): 100–106.

8. Richard Metters and Vicente Vargas, "Organizing Work in Service Firms," *Business Horizons* 43, no. 4 (July–August 2000): 23–32.

9. Clayton M. Christensen and Scott D. Anthony, "Cheaper, Faster, Easier: Disruption in the Service Sector," *Strategy and Innovation* 2, no. 1 (January–February 2004): 56–65.

10. Leonard L. Berry, *On Great Service* (New York: Free Press, 1995), 133.

11. Jeffrey Pfeffer, *Competitive Advantage Through People: Unleashing the Power of the Work Force* (Boston: Harvard Business School Press, 1994), 30–59.

12. Frances X. Frei, "The Four Things a Service Business Must Get Right," *Harvard Business Review* 86, no. 4 (April 2008): 70–80.

13. Richard B. Chase and Sriram Dasu, "Want to Perfect Your Company's Service? Use Behavioral Science," *Harvard Business Review* 79, no. 6 (June 2001): 78–84.

Chapter 8

1. This chapter draws not only on my own experience but also on the excellent contributions of Jean Harvey, *Managing Service Delivery Processes* (Milwaukee: ASQ Quality Press, 2006), and James L. Heskett, W. Earl Sasser, Jr., and Christopher W. L. Hart, *Service Breakthroughs* (New York: Free Press, 1990).

2. Michael E. Porter, "What Is Strategy?" *Harvard Business Review* 74, no. 6 (November–December 1996): 69.

3. For more on segments of opportunity and how they are created, see Anthony W. Ulwick, *What Customers Want* (New York: McGraw-Hill, 2005). Customer jobs are the preferred segmentation input if the company's goal is to discover new

market opportunities. Customer outcomes are the preferred segmentation input if the company's goal is to discover segments within a market—perhaps for a particular service.

4. Leonard L. Berry, *On Great Service* (New York: Free Press, 1995), 71.

5. They are able to do this because they understand the true costs of poor service quality, and they understand that higher service quality and productivity go hand in hand. See Heskett, Sasser, and Hart, *Service Breakthroughs*.

6. Frances X. Frei, "The Four Things a Service Business Must Get Right," *Harvard Business Review* 86 no. 4 (April 2008): 70–80.

7. Personal communication, February 25, 2009.

8. Valarie Zeithaml, Mary Jo Bitner, and Dwayne Gremler, *Services Marketing: Integrating Customer Focus Across the Firm,* 5th ed. (New York: McGraw-Hill, 2009), 265.

9. For an excellent discussion of service blueprinting, see Mary Jo Bitner, Amy L. Ostrom, and Felicia N. Morgan, "Service Blueprinting: A Practical Technique for Service Innovation," *California Management Review* 50, no. 3 (Spring 2008): 66–94.

10. It is beyond the scope of this book to discuss these topics in detail. However, they are well covered in several services marketing and management books, including Zeithaml, Bitner, and Gremler, *Services Marketing.*

11. The causes of ineffective service can be discovered using the universal job map steps of Chapter 6 even if the company has not mapped the provider job. The universal job map can also be used to create a service blueprint that isolates potential failure points in the current service delivery process, based on customers' outcome opportunities.

12. It is certainly possible that this process reveals some concepts or bundles of features that could form the basis for new services. It is important to discuss these ideas separately to shape them into complete concepts.

13. The universal job map for providing service (Figure 6-1) can be used for this purpose even when no service currently exists to help get the job done.

14. To assess impact, each of the individual steps in providing service may be rated for its impact on all of the high-opportunity outcomes. Using a simple scale—such as no impact (zero points), low impact (one point), medium impact (three points), and high impact (nine points)—the impact of each provider step can be calculated by summing the points across all high-opportunity outcomes.

15. In a similar manner, different service delivery approaches and offerings can be identified by theme among the opportunities rather than steps in the job. The rest of the process proceeds in the same way.

16. For more on service development, see Robert G. Cooper and Scott J. Edgett, *Product Development for the Service Sector* (New York: Basic Books, 1999).

Conclusion

1. Stephen L. Vargo and Robert F. Lusch, "Evolving to a New Dominant Logic for Marketing," *Journal of Marketing* 68, no. 1 (January 2004), 1–17.

2. Evert Gummesson, "Relationship Marketing: Its Role in the Service Economy," in *Understanding Services Management*, edited by W. J. Glynn and J. G. Barnes (New York: Wiley, 1995), 250.

3. Reena Jana, "Service Innovation: The Next Big Thing," *BusinessWeek*, March 29, 2007. Available at www. businessweek.com/innovate/content/mar2007/ id20070329_376916.htm.

4. A focus on the job a customer is trying to accomplish recognizes that customers are often coproducers of value, even when they hire goods. This also aligns with the service-dominant logic of marketing.

BIBLIOGRAPHY

Berry, Leonard L. *On Great Service.* New York: Free Press, 1995.
———, and Neeli Bendapudi. "Clueing in Customers." *Harvard Business Review* 81, no. 2 (February 2003): 100–106.
———, and Kent D. Seltman. "Building a Strong Services Brand: Lessons from Mayo Clinic." *Business Horizons* 50, no. 3 (March 2007): 199–209.
Bettencourt, Lance A. "Debunking Myths About Customer Needs." *Marketing Management* (January–February 2009): 46–52.
———, Amy L. Ostrom, Stephen W. Brown, and Robert I. Roundtree. "Client Co-Production in Knowledge-Intensive Business Services." *California Management Review* 44, no. 4 (Summer 2002): 100–128.
———, and Anthony W. Ulwick. "The Customer-Centered Innovation Map." *Harvard Business Review* 86, no. 5 (May 2008): 109–114.
Bitner, Mary Jo, Amy L. Ostrom, and Felicia N. Morgan. "Service Blueprinting: A Practical Technique for Service Innovation." *California Management Review* 50, no. 3 (Spring 2008): 66–94.

Booms, Bernard H., and Mary Jo Bitner. "Marketing Strategies and Organizational Structures for Service Firms." In *Marketing of Services,* edited by J. H. Donnelly and W. R. George. Chicago: American Marketing Association, 1981, 47–51.

Brown, Stephen W., Anders Gustafsson, and Lars Witell. "Beyond Products." *Wall Street Journal,* June 22, 2009. Available at online.wsj.com/article/SB10001424052970204 830304574131273123644620.html.

Chase, Richard B., and Sriram Dasu. "Want to Perfect Your Company's Service? Use Behavioral Science." *Harvard Business Review* 79, no. 6 (June 2001): 78–84.

Chesbrough, Henry. "Toward a New Science of Services." *Harvard Business Review* 83, no. 2 (February 2005): 43–44.

Chopra, Sunil, and Martin A. Lariviere. "Managing Service Inventory to Improve Performance." *MIT Sloan Management Review* 47, no. 1 (Fall 2005): 56–63.

Christensen, Clayton M., and Scott D. Anthony. "Cheaper, Faster, Easier: Disruption in the Service Sector." *Strategy and Innovation* 2, no. 1 (January–February 2004): 56–65.

Cooper, Robert G., and Scott J. Edgett. *Product Development for the Service Sector.* New York: Basic Books, 1999.

Cory, Jim. "Bird's-Eye View." *Replacement Contractor Magazine,* May 14, 2009. Available at www.replacementcontractor online.com/industry-news-print.asp?sectionID=0&arti cleID=958433.

Eder, Rob, and Antoinette Alexander. "Chains Put Pharmacy First in Strategic Initiatives." *Drug Store News,* August 18, 2003. Available at findarticles.com/p/articles/mi_m3374/ is_10_25/ai_108969618/.

Frei, Frances X. "Breaking the Trade-off Between Efficiency and Service." *Harvard Business Review* 84, no. 11 (November 2006): 92–101.

————. "The Four Things a Service Business Must Get Right."
    Harvard Business Review 86, no. 4 (April 2008): 70–80.
Gummesson, Evert. "Relationship Marketing: Its Role in the
    Service Economy." In *Understanding Services Management*,
    edited by W. J. Glynn and J. G. Barnes. New York: Wiley,
    1995, 244–268.
Harvey, Jean. *Managing Service Delivery Processes*. Milwaukee:
    ASQ Quality Press, 2006.
Heskett, James L. "Lessons in the Service Sector." *Harvard Business Review* 65, no. 2 (March–April 1987): 118–126.
————, W. Earl Sasser, Jr., and Christopher W. L. Hart. *Service
    Breakthroughs*. New York: Free Press, 1990.
Honebein, Peter. *Strategies for Effective Customer Education*. Chicago: American Marketing Association, 1997.
Jana, Reena. "Service Innovation: The Next Big Thing." *Business-Week*, March 29, 2007. Available at www.businessweek.
    com/innovate/content/mar2007/id20070329_376916.htm.
Kotler, Philip, and Gary Armstrong. *Principles of Marketing*.
    Upper Saddle River, NJ: Prentice-Hall, 1999.
Lovelock, Christopher. *Product Plus*. New York: McGraw-Hill,
    1994.
MacMillan, Ian C., and Rita Gunther McGrath. "Discovering
    New Points of Differentiation." *Harvard Business Review*
    75, no. 4 (July–August 1997): 133–145.
McAfee, Andrew, and Erik Brynjolfsson. "Dog Eat Dog." *Wall
    Street Journal*, April 27, 2007. Available at sloanreview.mit.
    edu/business-insight/articles/2007/2/4925/dog-eat-
    dog/.
Metters, Richard, and Vicente Vargas. "Organizing Work in Service Firms." *Business Horizons* 43, no. 4 (July–August
    2000): 23–32.

Ouren, John. "Marketers and Researchers Must Do More to Ensure Real Respondents." *CustomerThink.com*, February 6, 2009. Available at www.customerthink.com/article/researchers_must_ensure_real_respondents.

Pfeffer, Jeffrey. *Competitive Advantage Through People*. Boston: Harvard Business School Press (HBSP), 1994.

Pine, B. Joseph II, and James H. Gilmore. *The Experience Economy*. Boston: Harvard Business School Press (HBSP), 1999.

Porter, Michael E. "What Is Strategy?" *Harvard Business Review* 74, no. 6 (November-December 1996): 61–78.

Slywotzky, Adrian, Richard Wise, and Karl Weber. *How to Grow When Markets Don't*. New York: Warner Business Books, 2003.

Tax, Stephen S., Mark Colgate, and David E. Bowen. "How to Prevent Your Customers from Failing." *MIT Sloan Management Review* 47, no. 4 (Spring 2006): 30–38.

Thomke, Stefan. "R&D Comes to Services: Bank of America's Pathbreaking Experiments." *Harvard Business Review* 81, no. 4 (April 2003): 70–79.

Ulwick, Anthony W. "Turn Customer Input into Innovation." *Harvard Business Review* 80, no. 1 (January 2002): 91–97.

———. *What Customers Want*. New York: McGraw-Hill, 2005.

———, and Lance A. Bettencourt. "Giving Customers a Fair Hearing." *MIT Sloan Management Review* 49, no. 3 (Spring 2008): 62–68.

Vargo, Stephen L., and Robert F. Lusch. "Evolving to a New Dominant Logic for Marketing." *Journal of Marketing* 68, no. 1 (January 2004): 1–17.

Zeithaml, Valarie, Mary Jo Bitner, and Dwayne Gremler. *Services Marketing: Integrating Customer Focus Across the Firm*, 5th ed. New York: McGraw-Hill, 2009.

INDEX

ABOUT THE AUTHOR

Lance Bettencourt is a strategy adviser with Strategyn, Inc., the pioneer of outcome-driven innovation. Since joining Strategyn in 2003, he has served as a consultant to Microsoft, Hewlett-Packard, Ceridian, TD Bank Financial Group, Abbott Medical Optics, and several other leading corporations. Prior to joining Strategyn, he served on the marketing faculty at Arizona State University and Indiana University. He lives in Bloomington, Indiana, with his family.